ISBN 978-0-259-09729-7
PIBN 10796859

1 MONTH OF
FREE
READING

at
www.ForgottenBooks.com

By purchasing this book you are eligible for one month membership to ForgottenBooks.com, giving you unlimited access to our entire collection of over 700,000 titles via our web site and mobile apps.

To claim your free month visit:

www.forgottenbooks.com/free796859

HANEY'S USEFUL HANDBOOKS.

THE

IMPROMPTU
SPEAKER,

OR,

WHAT TO SAY WHEN CALLED ON.

PRICE TWENTY-FIVE CENTS.

NEW YORK:
JESSE HANEY AND COMPANY PUBLI

Haney's Art of Training Animals.

This book is a complete guide to the amateur or professional trainer, exhibiting all the secrets and mysteries of the craft, and showing how all circus tricks, and all feats of all performing animals—from elephants to fleas—are accomplished. It also has an improved system of horse and colt breaking, care and tuition of song, talking and performing birds, snake charming, bee taming, and many other things, making a large, handsome volume of over 200 pages, and over 60 illustrations. It is a wonderful book, and a vastly popular one. It tells everything connected with the art of training animals, is the recognized authority among professionals, and is a perfect treasure to any boy or to any person having animals, for it teaches many things useful and profitable to every farmer and animal owner. **50 cts**

Secrets Worth Knowing.—A guide to the manufacture of hundreds of useful and salable articles, including patent medicines, perfumery, toilet and dental articles, and many others easily made at trifling cost and selling readily at large profit. Many of these recipes are sold singly for several times the cost of our entire book. **25 cts**

Guide to Authorship.—A practical instructor in all kinds of literary composition, with all kinds of useful information on such points as writers, whether experienced or not, generally desire assistance. It includes punctuation, proof-reading, editing, preparation of MS., and its value and disposal, copyrights and customs in the trade, publishing and estimates for getting up books, pamphlets, sheet music, etc., with a vast amount of sensible and valuable information, just what writers want, and will save them time and money ; to be had nowhere else. **50 cts**

Phonographic Handbook.—An entirely new work for self-instruction in the modern improved system, used by practical reporters in the courts of law and on the newspapers. It unites simplicity with thoroughness. **25 cts**

Rogues and Rogueries.—An exposure of the snares and pitfalls of the great metropolis, and the multitude of devices for entrapping the unwary, including many of the operations practiced in other cities, and swindles through the mail. New, revised, and enlarged illustrated edition. **25 cts**

Bad Memory Made Good and Good Made Better.—Shows how a wonderful power of memory may be acquired by a simple art, readily learned, and enabling its possessor to achieve feats incomprehensible to those ignorant of the secret. It will be of great assistance to teachers, pupils and professional men generally. Clergymen and speakers will save much time by its chapter on Speaking without Notes, as will students preparing for examination. **15 cts**

Comicalities, by Orpheus C. Kerr.—A capital work by this very popular American humorist. 150 illustrations. **25 cts**

Common Sense Cook Book.—One of the best, giving a vast number of best dishes, both elaborate and simple, to suit all tastes. **25 cts**

Hunting, Trapping, and Fishing Made Easy.—New, reliable and gives more matter than any dollar book. *double* the amount of any 25ct. book, including preparation and use of bait, traps, &c., all modes of preserving and preparing skins and furs, and much other practical and valuable information—just what is wanted. Price *lower* than *any* other; *none* (even at $2 or $5) *more* reliable ; none at less than $1, as reliable and complete. With fifty illustrations. **20 cts**

Painter's Manual.—Giving best methods and latest improvements in house painting, sign painting, graining, varnishing, polishing, staining, gilding, glazing, silvering, Grecian oil-painting, hinese painting, Oriental painting, etc. Also, principles of glass staining, harmony and contrast of colors, with philosophy, theories and practices of color, etc. Includes also Practical Paper Hanging. **50 cts**

Rapid Reckoning.—The Art of Performing Arithmetical Calculations almost instantaneously. Any one can learn and apply. The famous "Lightning Calculator's" exhibitions (same system) were the marvel of thousands. Secret was lately sold for $1. In book form, enlarged. **25 cts**

Haney's Handbook of Ventriloquism.—A complete and practical self-instructor, which the New York *Atlas* says is "so easy that a little practice will enable any one to produce the most wonderful vocal illusions." It gives numerous examples for practice and exhibition, many curious vocal illusions and instructions for imitating birds, animals, &c Also tells how to use and make the famous Magic Whistle. It is the *best* book at *lowest* price. The New York *Free Press* says : " The boys have so often been humbuged by advertised instructions in ventriloquism that they will be thankful to Mr. Haney for furnishing at such trifling cost a book from which the art can really be fully and easily learned by any one." **15 cts**

THE

IMPROMPTU SPEAKER;

OR,

WHAT TO SAY WHEN CALLED ON.

A GUIDE TO

EXTEMPORANEOUS SPEAKING OF ALL KINDS AND
ON ALL OCCASIONS, HINTS ON ETIQUETTE,
CUSTOMARY FORMS, &c.

BY THE AUTHOR OF THE GUIDE TO AUTHORSHIP.

NEW YORK:
JESSE HANEY AND COMPANY, PUBLISHERS,
No. 119 NASSAU STREET.

GOOD BOOKS FOR SELF-IMPROVEMENT.

PHONOGRAPHIC HANDBOOK.

A practical guide to learning the latest and most improved style of phonography as actually used by thousands of practical reporters in the courts, on newspapers and elsewhere. A knowledge of phonography not only affords remunerative employment by itself, but it may be made a useful and profitable addition in many professions and aid in securing desirable situations in many branches of business. Orr book is designed especially for *Self-Instruction.* **25** cents.

GUIDE TO AUTHORSHIP.

This book is invaluable to all who desire to write for the press, and is also useful to every one who has occasion for any literary effort whether in prose or verse. Some of the most practiced and successful writers have stated that they found hints which saved them much labor, while those just entering upon authorship will be spared many failures, disappointments and needless worry, by its aid. Ideas are essential to success, but the details and customs of the craft are no less necessary. The Guide to Authorship tells many things which might take years of anxious experience to learn. but being told, the young writer can immediately profit by. It gives rules and explanations of all kinds of composition, prose and verse, editing, proof-reading, punctuation, capitalizing, copyrights, preparation, value, and disposal of MSS , choice of subjects, how to overcome defects, best literary markets, rates of pay, estimates of cost of publishing books, &c., how to introduce books, music publishing, &c., &c. Though *not* a "school book," it will be found useful to pupils in all literary undertakings, and a great aid to teachers in criticizing and correcting. Clergymen and speakers will find some things of interest. **50** cents.

IMPROMPTU SPEAKER.

A guide to the proper remarks to make on all ordinary occasions and the etiquette of such occasions. It not only gives forms of speeches for those who prefer to adopt them, but teaches the reader how to be prepared when called on suddenly, that he may acquit himself creditably and without discomfort. **25** cents.

ARTISTS' MANUAL.

A Handbook of Oil Painting, designed for artists and amateurs. It is written by an American painter, some of whose pictures rank among the highest works of native art. It gives very full instructions on all points, especially items of practical value, embracing Portrait, Landscape. Figure and other branches of the art, with full details in regard to materials, manipulations, &c., and suggestions for economies for students and others. **50** cents. In press.

PUBLISHERS' PREFACE.

WHILE there are several works on the principles of oratory, and *collections* of speeches innumerable, it is believed that the specialty selected as the subject of the present work has been but barely, if at all, touched upon elsewhere. There are few of us who are not at some time called on to say a few words in public ; these demands may come when least expected. To be unable to say anything under such circumstances is not only humiliating to the individual himself, but may seem discourteous to those who have honored him by the call.

There are many having all natural qualifications demanded, who fail for the want of a few hints and helps. The difficulties experienced are often of an imaginary character, or of such trifling nature that an experienced speaker would have little comprehension of their crushing effect upon the novice. To point out the requirements of all ordinary occasions of impromptu speech-making, and to afford such aid as may be useful, are the aims of this little treatise. While avoiding formal rules and elaborate disquisitions, care will be taken to show clearly the things to avoid as well as the things to strive for, in both the matter and the manner of the speech, and the particular points of etiquette to be observed.

Occasionally persons of excessive diffidence, however fully they may know the requirements of the occasion or thoroughly prepared themselves for their discharge, fail for no other reason than this timidity. Such individuals will probably be glad to know that a most sensible chapter on "Gaining Confidence," giving much interesting and useful information as to the causes and most effective means of overcoming this distressing weakness, may be found in a little pamphlet entitled "Self-Cure of Stammering," which can be had of any bookseller at an outlay of twenty-five cents.

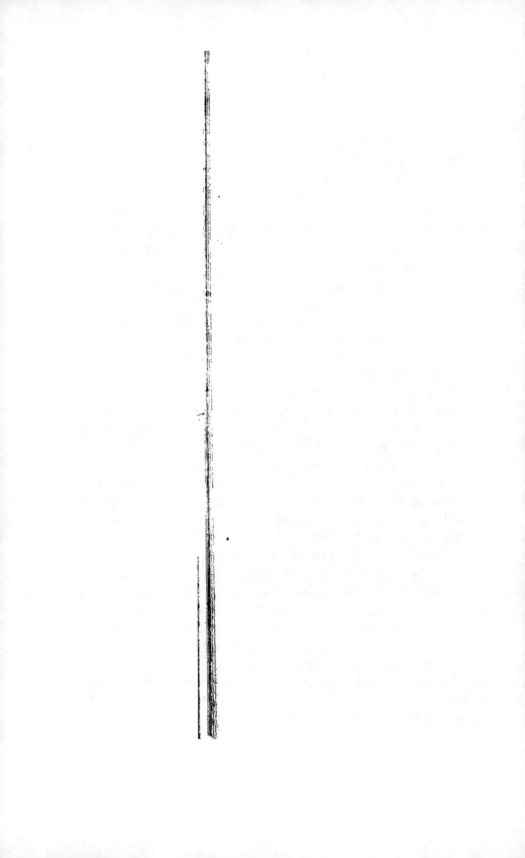

THE IMPROMPTU SPEAKER.

PART I.—INTRODUCTION.

ON very great public occasions, none save a very practiced speaker is apt to be called upon to address
others ; and a practiced speaker either needs no instruction
or from a confidence in his own powers is apt to spurn it.
But an ordinary man finds many periods of his life when he
is suddenly required to face an audience, and where he is
expected by those around him to say something.   On such
occasions we have witnessed a vast deal of embarrassment.
Men who could talk well enough on ordinary matters, and
who were fluent of speech among their fellows, found themselves tongue-tied, or fearfully hesitant, when expected to
stand on their legs, and talk to an audience of a dozen,
none of whom they regarded as their superiors.   It often
occurred to me that an essay upon extemporaneous
speakers, giving hints to those same bashful fellows how
to speak and act when necessity calls for speech and
action, might save a deal of trouble and annoyance to all
parties.   The publishers of this little manual, having the
same notion, applied to me to prepare them a short practical work on the subject, and this chiming with my own
views, I set about the task.   This much to show why this
little book has been prepared and published.

  It is not merely my purpose to give models of speeches
which may serve for imitation and guidance, or with modifi-
cations, might even be cribbed on many occasions, but
rather instead of teaching my readers how to use other
people's brains, to show them how they may cultivate their
own.   I wish to show them, whether the quick-witted or
dull, the principles that lie at the bottom of all manner of
speech making, and to teach, not only the kind of language to

be used, but the mode and manner of using it; the most
ordinary man, though he may not become a great orator
without close study and natural qualifications, may nevertheless learn to acquit himself creditably when occasion
calls for the utterance of a few well chosen words.

I am aware there is too much speech-making among us.
The tendency of the age is to gab. Vanity prompts men
to talk, and love of amusement, or a pernicious custom,
impels others to demand talk. But since it is a tendency
of our people, neither censure nor ridicule will break it
down. The only thing left is to render it as little offensive
as possible. Let us try to make those who will talk, even
in articulo mortis, talk sense, or that agreeable nonsense
which sometimes is its proper substitute. On most festive
occasions, the audience is a friendly one. They wish the
speaker to succeed. His failure is not even a satisfaction
to his enemies, if such should happen to be among the
guests, for it would mar the pleasure of the occasion so
much that the gratification of personal spite would not pay
for it. On all such occasions the party must endeavor
to remember that he is in his own house, in many respects,
and that he is really not making a speech at all.

In that fact lies, however, the genuine cause of all embarrassment inexperienced and unreflecting people suppose,
when they are called on to say anything, that they must
deliver themselves of something witty or profound or elegant. Wit, if it be real is always acceptable, but, unless
in a practiced hand, is a dangerous edged tool to handle.
Profundity and studied elegance are out of place at an
ordinary social gathering. A man who has to present
something to his friend, in the presence of common friends,
detracts from the value of the gift, if he bore the recipient
and the rest with a set oration. Neither the subject nor
the time justifies it. A studied piece of declamation ending
by the gift of a walking stick, or a silver mug is like the
cry of the street vender in Constantinople: "In the name
of Allah and the Prophet—figs!" The rule on this, as on
every other occasion, is to rise to the subject, and not above
it, and when you have done, to stop. The last is a rule
which some speakers think they should honor more by the

breach than the observance, and this false notion of theirs
is what makes the proceedings in town meetings, and the
debates in legislative bodies so dreary and tedious to the
listeners.

Inseparable from the mode of making small speeches is
the etiquette of such occasions. One half of the effect is
due to decorum. The speaker has to consider where he
is, and who is around him. He has to study ease of manner
and this is best studied by not thinking of it at all.

In rising to speak get up naturally and stand as you
always do, without any endeavor to strike a picturesque
attitude. Make no attempt to look solemn, or you will be
apt to look silly. Avoid gesture, which is only graceful
and effective when it springs from the excitement of the
moment in a long and animated discourse. Speak in your
natural tone of voice, neither too low or too high—lower at
first, and increasing your tone gradually as you go on.
Fix your eye on the farthest man, and speak so that he can
hear you easily, and then all the rest will.

Above all remember that on minor occasions you rise to
talk, and not to declaim ; and the nearer you approach to
the colloquial in what you say, the more you will please
your friends, and satisfy yourself.

PART II.—OF TABLE SPEAKING.

THE American people, like their English, Irish and Scotch
progenitors—to say nothing of the German element
—belong to an eating race ; and no gathering seems complete to them without an unlimited amount of food and
drink be furnished. The phrase, " dinner-speech," is
genuine, and may be made to include talking at a variety of
places, from a wedding-breakfast to a clam-bake. But the
dinner-speech proper is of a more formal nature than others
of the genus, and sometimes involves a little premedita-
tion.

The etiquette of a dinner in public differs very little from that of a dinner given by gentlemen of elegant habits and sufficient means to a select party of friends. But in the latter case the guests are usually those who are accustomed to dining out, and acquainted with its observances; at a public dinner-table, the guests are mixed. I do not speak of bores, who are noisy, call loudly to the waiters, and otherwise make asses of themselves; nor of people who insist upon eating peas with their knife, or suck up their soup with the noise of pigs eating from a trough. There are very worthy and estimable people who are guilty of none of these acts of table ruffianism, who conduct themselves quietly and decorously, and yet who are not well acquainted with the etiquette of the public dinner. They do not know when to rise, or when to sit down again; when to applaud or when to refrain from applauding, and frequently mar the pleasure of the occasion from the best intention in the world. They can be as easily taught in one lesson as in twenty.

Apropos to that, let me give a pleasant bit of experience of my own.

Some years since I was called on to preside over a dinner given upon a birth-day anniversary. The dinner was political, and the diners were mostly very honest, but not altogether polished working-men. Among the invited guests were the vice-president elect of the United States, afterward envoy to England, a gentleman distinguished for his elegant manners; several officers of the navy and army, a judge or two, and the recorder of a neighboring city. When I sent out the committee to conduct the guests to the room, I said a few words to those already at the table. I told them that one or two of them might not be well acquainted with certain forms, and in order that we might preserve proper decorum they were to rise when I raised my hand gently, sit when I depressed it, and watch my signal for applause. The next minute the committee announced at the door—"The vice-president elect of the United States, and suite." I rose, and every man at table rose at the same instant, and remained standing until the guests were seated. Then as I sunk into my seat the whole body of diners sank into theirs with the uniformity of a corp of soldiers. And so throughout. The most amusing thing to me was the precision of drinking the toasts. Every glass was raised to the mouth simultaneously with mine, and as I was at the head of the table, the effect of a long double row of glasses with the bottoms facing each other, was slightly ludicrous. But everything went off admirably, for every one looked to the chairman as bugleman. When the time came for our guests to leave, every man rose with me to his feet, all facing the line down which the guests passed. Afterward the vice-president said to me: "Your members must have been at a great many suppers in their time. I have witnessed a good many things of the kind, but I never saw one where the decorum was so perfect, and where everything went off so smoothly and naturally. I bowed, and kept my own counsel. It is twenty-seven years since then, but I have only to shut my eyes, and I can see as plainly as I did then, two rows of men, standing with only a table between them, and each apparently taking aim at the man opposite through the bottom of a wine-glass.

At all these public dinners, whether of a society, or for political purposes, set speakers of some note are provided, who respond to the most important toasts of the day, and it is only when these have concluded, and the wine has made a good many circuits around the table, that the guests clamor for talk from less conspicuous personages, and insist on every one who is of any prominence, or even has the reputation of being " a good fellow," adding his mite to the treasury of table eloquence. Men at this state of affairs are not apt to be critical; but they will not submit to long speeches. A response to a call, whether in the shape of a personal toast, or from being named generally, should be prompt, short and to the point.

Though you be called out by a personal toast, do not talk about yourself, or drag your business before the company, as many do. We were present once at the dinner of a horticultural society, where, for some reason, or through want of reason, an undertaker and sexton was called on to speak; we remember what he said, almost word for word, and it was as follows :

"I don't know why, Mr. President, I am called on to talk. I am an undertaker, but I never undertook to make a speech, unless I was overtaken by liquor, and I assure you I am quite sober. On such an occasion all the talking ought to be lively, and from lively people. I am not lively, and never have a lively time of it, except when other people go out. I never go out, except professionally. I take no pleasure, though as I had a negro funeral last week, I may say that I went a black burying for half a day. I can not make a speech as you see, but I am much obliged to you for drinking my health—(please don't drink the good health of too many people or you might ruin me)— and I will be happy to serve any of you in the way of my profession— (Cries of "Oh! no!" "Not for me; thank you!" etc.) I don't mean in any way but to give you pleasure—say for instance, if any one of you has the great misfortune to lose his mother-in-law."

Now this was all funny in its way, but it was in very bad taste. A short speech at the same dinner—made in despair by a very bashful fellow, was accidentally better. He rose, and after a little hesitancy said:

"I am very much obliged to you, gentlemen, for drinking my good health; but I neither intend to return the compliment in kind, for in drinking the health of every man here, I should lose my own; nor to try to make a speech, for in that case, I should lose my reputation as a man of judgment."

Down he sat, and that was the end of it. He said nothing very brilliant, but he at least did no discredit to himself.

There are those who have a great aptitude for saying either humorous or brilliant things in an easy, natural and off-hand way, and in consequence are much sought after for public dinners. A word here in the ear of the reader, in strict confidence—most of the apropos affairs, especially the happy extemporaneous hits, have been carefully studied before hand. No matter for that, so they are dexterously fitted to the place and to the occasion. But if a man cultivate an easy and natural way of talking—if he practice saying things without attempt to astonish or impress, he will be apt in the end to astonish himself and impress an audience. The good company, the genial feeling, and the flow of spirits of all around him—to say nothing of the flow of wine—will bring out all the dormant powers. The first effort is to forget that he is making a speech at all. We insist on this, at the risk of offending by repetition, since it is the key to good speaking on any occasion

The breakfast speech, little known on this side of the Atlantic, differs essentially from the dinner and supper speech. It is a cold-blooded affair. The dinner speech springs from the companionship, the wine and the geniality of the occasion—the breakfast speech comes from the occasion itself. The dinner speech may arise unexpectedly; the breakfast speech is made with malice aforethought. Breakfasts at which there are a number of guests outside of the family are mostly given in this country on the occasion of weddings. A merry couple having been properly tied together, and legally authorized to pull different ways in harness for the rest of their joint lives, prepare to travel away for a time, in order to let everybody in the rail-way cars, and at strange hotels, know that they are bride and groom. Before they go they feed generally in company with their friends—that is, the bridegroom feeds, it being strict etiquette for the bride to take only the rations of a hen-sparrow. She may pick a grain of rice, like Amina, or even eat a pea, like Beau Brummel, but no more, since her modesty and blushes are supposed to stand instead of beefsteaks and potatoes. Speeches are in order, of course. Every one feels the whole affair is silly, and that he cuts a ridiculous figure. Hence he finds refuge from his own annoyance in gabbling himself, or causing others to gabble. The bridegroom is toasted, and he replies—generally with something about " the happiest day of my life "—" unequal to the occasion "—" thanks not to be expressed "—and so on. The bride is toasted, and somebody else replies for her—generally, the groomsman, or " best man "—as they call him of late. The father of the bride is toasted, the mother is toasted—everybody is toasted in turn; and all these people by themselves or deputy reply. As there is little to talk about there is generally little said, though they usually employ a good many words to say it in.

Any one is liable to be called out on such occasions, and everybody usually is. As the breakfast is given just before departure, and the railway train stops to wait for no one, but vigorously sets off according to the time-table; as the trunk, basket, little box, big box, band-box and bundle have been already checked by one of the groomsman; there

is none too much time for the speeches. The breakfast
eloquence has to be fired off like the rifles of sharpshooters,
rapidly and effectively ; but the bore of the orational rifle
should be as little as possible.

Supper-speeches are another variation of table talk ; but
these and dinner-speeches are essentially the same. There
are exceptions, however, the two most notable of which are
the ball-supper speech, and that made to the proprietor of
the house at a surprise party. The speech at a ball-supper
should be particularly light, frothy and lively, or not at
all. People go to a ball, or a party, to enjoy themselves,
and not to air their learning, their profundity, or their eloquence. A supper-speech there, as elsewhere, should have
a point, like an epigram, should be brief, like an epigram,
and when its point is made, it should stop, like an epigram. I just now remember of a speech of the kind. A
few years since Julius Schuberth, the well-known music
publisher, gave an invitation supper and musical party on
the occasion of the house of which he was head and founder
having reached its fiftieth anniversary. It was a very
pleasant evening— several quite eminent artists rendered
some music charmingly, and the old man himself gave one
of his own compositions with spirit and taste. The colla-
tion was excellent too, and evidently every one present was
pleased. As the wine began to flow, some speeches were
made in German and English, complimenting the host of
the evening, and he was called on for a response. Now the
old gentleman could render his feelings very well in a
rhythmical way, but was not equal to the task through
plain prose ; and he requested, through a common friend,
that a well known literary gentleman then present, and who
had taken no apparent interest in the proceedings should
reply for him. The gentleman, to whom the summons was
unexpected—he had never seen Schuberth before, though
he knew his history, rose, and said, as nearly as we recollect :

"Mr. Schuberth distrusts his own power of expression, or possibly
feels that his emotions will not allow him to use language fitting the
occasion; and he has asked me to return thanks for all the kind words
used in his honor, and for the kind feeling which shows as much even

in your manner as the words. I shall not attempt to do it. There is an eloquence in his eyes that needs no words to interpret it. Besides why should you be thanked for what you cannot help? You are most of you either musicians or lovers of music. In honoring one who has during his long connection with the trade done so much to elevate the standard of taste, and to reconcile purism with progress, you honor the art you love, and so honor yourselves. Mr. Schuberth for half a century has been at the head of a house, which has given the public the best productions of the best masters, and has never through a love of gain lent its imprint to what was false to taste or impure in morals. Your presence to-night it would have been impossible to refuse. The date is an epoch. The occasion is a festivity. It is more. You are not here to flatter the successful publisher, or to pay a tribute to the man who has possibly amassed a competence. Fifty years since Papa Schuberth was married to art, and you are here to celebrate his golden wedding."

The other exceptional table-speech is that of the surprise party. When you have impertinently taken possession of a man's house for the purpose of a frolic, you have to temper your act of social ruffianism by a faint effort to practice some of the amenities of life. You must at least say something to tickle the vanity of the man you have injured. Always presuming that your host is a fool, and, being a fool, does not set his dog on to bite you, or does not have yourself and your confederates removed by the police, it becomes your duty to utter a few pleasant sayings. There are some people who, after they have got up a surprise party, and have turned a man's house upside down, have the temerity and bad taste to clap him on the back with the brutal exclamation—"High old time, Jonesy, my boy!" or the impertinent inquiry—"How are you enjoying yourself, old fellow?" The artistic and æsthetic surprise-party brigand acts better. He waits until the party is half drunk, and the mortification and impotent rage of the master of the house has somewhat deadened, and then he calls for attention, and enters, for the benefit of the few who will listen, into a panegyric upon the unwilling host. And if he do this with dexterity, if he lay on the flattery thickly, and deliver his remarks with unction, and a " bless you, mi-dear-boy!" air, the victim in spite of his better judgment will begin to believe that his visitors loved him so well they could not stay away, instead of recognizing the fact that they had merely taken his premises instead of a public hall because they could be had without payment.

The birth-day speech is generally a stereotyped affair, in which there can be little varity. By this we mean the speech to the person whose birth-day is to be celebrated, or his reply. The other speeches fall under the general rule of table talk.

We have said that it is in bad taste in general to allude, in dinner-speeches to the business, the profession or the peculiarities of those around you. It is also in bad taste, and frequently offensive, to play upon the names of parties, These rules have, however, their exceptions. Where those present are nearly all of one business, allusions if pleasantly made are proper enough, and may add much to the satisfaction of the guests; and where all are intimate a gay pun on the name of some one present may be pardonable. Still such things require caution. We remember a very pleasant evening once, where the speeches were generally of this exceptional kind. It was an occasion of a farewell supper given to the senior member of a firm of leather-dealers, previous to his departure for a year's visit to Europe, and nearly all present were either in the hide and leather trade, or connected therewith in some way.

The gentleman who on this occasion proposed the complimentary toast to the host of the evening, after the usual compliments and good wishes, wound up by saying:

"And we have no doubt that our good friend, as he passes through the old cities of the world, rubbing here against a noble, and jostling there against a peasant, will so conduct himself after his usual well-bred and quiet fashion, that all ranks and classes will admit, that, for the purpose of making a really estimable man, there is nothing like leather. In fact, leather is a type of your perfect man It is smooth, but not too oily; it is pliable, but does not give way; it bends when needed, but does not crack—it wears well—it is in fact, an educated skin, altogether different from the original stiff and unpleasant hide."

In replying the traveler-to-be said:

"If I deserved one half of the pleasant things said on this occasion, I should think more of myself than I do; and I do think more of myself than I did when I first sat down to supper, because I know my friends are sincere in what they say, and I must be a pretty good sort of fellow, or they never would let their partiality get the better of their judgment as they have to-night. If I don't thank them and you for the friendship and kindly sympathy you show, it is because I have no words to do it so well as it deserves to be done; because no words can express my feelings, My hope is that when I get back that I will meet you each and all, and find the friendship which binds us to-night, and has bound us for years, made stronger and warmer by the absence. I ought to stop just here! and, so far as I am concerned, I do; but the gentleman who has just spoken has made a remark that might be almost thought a personal allusion to one of my partners in business— a gentleman who though he is the Co. in the firm, and was christened Jeremiah, no one wishes at Jericho. He is a little rough at times, but not stiff; and if he will only get on his feet and say something, will show you that he is by no means an unpleasant Hyde."

There was a general shout for Hyde, and that gentleman rose with great deliberation.

" Gentlemen," he said, " my partner, before he goes off on his year's holiday, is disposed to balance our books, and credits me with a little too much. I admit my stiffness, rather than my roughness. The fact is I am not so oily as either of these gentlemen. I am a Hyde that has never been tanned and curried As to there being nothing like leather, there would be nothing of leather, if you didn't have a Hyde to begin with."

There was a deal more said by various parties, but these quotations are enough to show that speeches filled with personal allusions may be made without offense, though the experiment is always hazardous, and generally in bad taste.

There is generally a certain amount of flippancy in successful dinner speeches, which causes them to appear badly in print. They lack in that shape, the spice, dash and geniality which surrounded them when delivered. But all such speeches are not flippant, and sometimes flippancy is out of place. A public dinner or supper is often given in aid of some noted charity, or on the anniversary of a society founded for a serious purpose. In that case the speeches, from that of the President on taking the chair down to that upon "woman," should have a certain amount of dignity along with the humors, and decorum with the wit. Mr. Charles Dickens, who was an exceedingly good dinner speaker of the English style, which is less free-and-easy than the American, got the just medium in the matter very well; and the following address of his when presiding at the annual festival of the London Newsvenders and Provident Institution, will serve as a fair model to study:

" When I had the honor of being asked to preside last year, I was prevented by indisposition, and I besought my friend, Mr. Wilkie Collins, to reign in my stead. He very kindly complied, and made an excellent speech. Now I tell you the truth, that I read that speech with considerably uneasiness, for it inspired me with a strong misgiving that I had better have presided last year with neuralgia in my face and my subject in my head, rather than preside this year with my neuralgia all gone and my subject anticipated. Therefore, I wish to preface the toast this evening by making the managers of this Institution one very solemn and repentant promise, and it is, if ever I find myself obliged to provide a substitute again they may rely upon my sending the most speechless man of my acquaintance.

"The chairman last year presented you with an amiable view of the universality of the newsman's calling. Nothing, I think, is left for me but to imagine the newsman's burden itself, to unfold one of those wonderful sheets which he every day disseminates, and to take a bird's eye view of its general character and contents. So, if you please, choosing my own time—though the newsman can not choose his time, for he must be equally active in winter or summer, in sunshine or sleet, in light or darkness, early or late—but, choosing my own time, I shall for two or three moments start off with the newsman on a fine May morning, and take a view of the wonderful broadsheets which every day he scatters broadcast over the country. Well, the first thing that occurs to me following the newsman is, that every day we are born, that every day we are married—some of us—and that every day we are dead; consequently, the first thing the newsvender's column informs me is, that Atkins has been born, that Catkins has been married, and that Datkins is dead But the most remarkable thing I immediately discover in the next column is, that Atkins has grown to be seventeen years old, and that he has run away; for, at last, my eye lights on the fact that William A., who is seventeen years old, is adjured immediately to return to his disconsolate parents, and every thing will be arranged to the satisfaction of every one. · I am afraid he will never return, simply because, if he had meant to come back, he would never have gone away. Immediately below, I find a mysterious character in such a mysterious difficulty that it is only to be expressed by several disjointed letters, by several figures, and several stars; and then I find the explanation in the intimation that the writer has given his property over to his uncle, and that the elephant is on the wing. Then, still glancing over the shoulder of my industrious friend, the newsman, I find there are great fleets of ships bound to all parts of the earth, that they all want a little more stowage, a little more cargo, that they have a few more berths to let, that they have all the most spacious decks, that they are all built of teak, and copper-bottomed, that they all carry surgeons of experience, and that they are all A 1 at Lloyds, and anywhere else. Still glancing over the shoulder of my friend the newsman, I find I am offered all kinds of house-lodging, clerks, servants, and situations, which I can possibly or impossibly want. I learn, to my intense gratification, that I need never grow old, that I may always preserve the juvenile bloom of my complexion; that if ever I turn ill it is entirely my own fault; that if I have any complaint, and want brown cod-liver oil or Turkish baths, I am told where to get them, and that, if I want an income of seven pounds a week, I may have it by sending half a crown in postage-stamps. Then I look to the police intelligence, and I can discover that I may bite off a human living nose cheaply, but if I take off the dead nose of a pig or a calf from a shop-window, it will cost me exceedingly dear. I also find if I allow myself to be betrayed into the folly of killing an inoffensive tradesman on his own door-step, that little incident will not affect the testimonials to my character, but that I shall be described as a most amiable young man, and as, above all things, remarkable for the singular inoffensiveness of my character and disposition. Then I turn my eye to the Fine Arts, and, under that head, I see that a certain ' J. O.' has most triumphantly exposed a certain ' J. O. B.' which ' J. O. B.' was remarkable for this particular ugly feature, that I was requested to deprive myself of the best of my pictures for six months; that for that time it was to be hung on a wet wall, and that I was to be requited for my courtesy in having my picture most impertinently covered with a wet blanket. To sum up the results of a glance over my newsman's shoulder, it gives a comprehensive knowledge of what is going on over the continent of Europe, and also of what is going on over the continent of America, to say nothing of such little geographical regions as India and China.

"Now, my friends, this is the glance over the newsman's shoulders from the whimsical point of view, which is the point, I believe, that most promotes digestion. The newsman is to be met with on steamboats, railway stations, and at every turn. His profits are small, he has a great amount of anxiety and care, and no little amount of personal wear and tear. He is indispensable to civilization and freedom, and he is looked for with pleasurable excitement every day, except when he lends the paper for an hour, and when he is punctual in calling for it, which is sometimes very painful. I think the lesson we can learn from our newsman is some new illustrations of the uncertainty of life, some illustration of its vicissitudes and fluctuations. Mindful of this permanent lesson, some members of the trade originated this society, which affords them assistance in time of sickness and indigence. The subscription is infinitesimal. It amounts annually to five shillings. Looking at the returns before me, the progress of the society would seem to be slow, but it has only been slow for the best of all reasons, that it has been sure.

"The pensions granted are all obtained from the interest on the funded capital, and, therefore, the Institution is literally as safe as the Bank. It is stated that there are several newsvenders who are not members of this society; but that is true in all institutions which have come under my experience. The persons who are most likely to stand in need of the benefits which an institution confers, and usually the persons to keep away until bitter experience comes to them too late."

PART III.—OF POLITICAL SPEECHES.

THERE are about two thousand counties, more or less, in the United States. In each of these there are held in a year at least ten political meetings on one side, and every fourth year twice as many. At these meetings the average number of speeches are three to each. The opposite party does the same amount of meeting and talking. Here we have the alarming spectacle of some one hundred and twenty thousand speeches let off annually for three years, and two hundred and fifty thousand fired into the air on the fourth year; being three-fifths of a million of speeches inflicted upon suffering American humanity in the space of forty-eight calendar months. I neither complain of this as an outrage, nor boast of it as showing both the great talking power of one part of my countrymen, and the capacity of enduring torture of the rest. I merely state the fact.

Now there can be no question that while there are a fair number of the speeches thus delivered that may be listened to with comfort and even with satisfaction, the greater part of this political eloquence is of a very low order of merit, or devoid of all merit whatever. And this state of affairs occurs, not from lack of brains on the part of political speakers, as from a lack of knowledge on the part of the auditors what a political speech should be. Instead of a careful discussion of public measures, the public expect to hear an attack upon men; instead of an appeal to their understanding, a mere attempt to pander to their prejudices. or amuse them for the moment. What they are supposed to want they get. If they considered that politics is merely, in its legitimate sense, a dispute about the proper mode of managing public affairs, and conducting public business, they would demand the views of their orators on topics of public interest connected with the management of public affairs. In truth, the greater part of people prefer good sense in a public speech to nonsense, and the speaker who will confine himself to his topic, enlivening it in a legitimate way, will secure more general approval than he who indulges in lofty flights, or who stoops to buffoonery in order to gain laughter and applause.

If you are called on to address a political meeting, or have a desire to mingle in that way in political affairs, the first point is to have something to say. And to have something to say it is necessary that you should be master of the subject. The preparation for speaking should be thorough—not in words, but in facts and ideas. As a good political speech is always short, you should confine yourself to one, or at most two branches of your subject. That is, you should speak on but one or two topics; but, as you cannot tell what those who speak before you will touch upon, you must be prepared on all.

If you are a novice, so soon as you have made yourself master of everything connected with the political campaign, after you have filled your mind full of the shameful omissions and criminal commissions of the opposite side, and mastered the policy which is proposed or sustained by your own party, it will be a good plan to write out a short speech upon any particular branch of the subject. Write this with great care, and condense it by striking out every adjective where it is possible and every phrase where the same idea or fact is repeated a second time. When you have got it to suit you, read it over and over until it is tolerably well fixed in your mind — not committed to memory—and then burn it as soon as possible. Having done that, read over any selection of speeches, including those given in this little hand-book—observe their style and the manner in which the speakers have handled the subject, throw them aside, and begin to write another speech, which, after completing and fixing in your mind, you will destroy like its predecessor. Then refresh your memory by reading up all the facts previously obtained. Understand that the best preparation for the discussion of any subject, political or otherwise, is to understand it thoroughly in all its shapes; and a continual written discussion of its salient points will confirm and fix the knowledge acquired by reading, or by listening to the remarks of well-informed persons.

Nor, to make an effective political speaker, is it alone necessary that you should be well acquainted with the differences between political parties. You should have a thorough knowledge of the political history of the country, the origin of parties, the different plans of finance, the opposing schemes of government, and a fair acquaintance with the administration of public affairs in other countries.

Having made yourself master of your subject, and fixed the knowledge more firmly in your mind by writing upon it, the next thing is to accustom yourself to an audience. To do this with the least embarrassment to yourself, and with the best chances for success, make your debut in some strange place. This is for two reasons—one, because there will be no familiar faces to divert your mind from its proper current of thought; and the other since, if you fail it is less mortifying to do so before strangers, while if you succeed your gratification will be as great there as anywhere. As "a prophet is not without honor, save in his own country," you will meet with more consideration abroad. You go there to teach, and they expect you to teach, and are prepared to hear favorably what you have to say. But in your own place the people know you, and not knowing you as a speaker, look with half amusement and half disgust at your attempt to talk to them; and the words—"Is Saul among the prophets?" stand out all over them in the most annoying way.

When you rise to address the people do it in the simplest and most unpretending way. If you can stand on the same level with your audience, they being seated, do so, or as little above them as possible. Nothing is more difficult than speaking from a hight. You have in that case to force your voice downward, when the sound naturally ascends. Begin slowly, and in a rather low tone of voice, about your usual pitch in talking out of-doors. Speak distinctly, and utter every syllable and sound clearly, and you will be heard where a hasty speaker twice as loud in voice would neither be heard nor understood. Speak in

NOTE.—Those desirous of detailed instructions in *writing* speeches, will find a chapter specially devoted to that subject in the "Guide to Authorship," which will afford great aid. Besides this chapter there are others which, though intended for *writers* rather than *speakers*, will yet be found very useful to the latter. An outlay of fifty cents for the "Guide" will, we think, prove a good investment on the part of all interested.

that earnest and natural tone which denotes you mean what you say.

As to the subject best suited to impress your audience, that depends upon circumstances. Sometimes a particular part of party policy becomes the object of attack, or the subject of defense, and it may be policy to talk of that and nothing else. As a general rule however, a political speaker should never defend, but always attack. The one who attacks, assails; the one who defends assumes the criminal's place. Take it for granted that you are right—you are there to show up the short-comings of your opponent.

Of course it depends a deal on which party you belong to. If you belong to the party in power, you see the action of the administration through rose-colored spectacles. Everything is lovely, and as it ought to be. If you are of the opposition, then you look at affairs through yellow glasses. Everything is doleful, and as it ought not to be. If the first, you point with pride to the fact that a large portion of the national debt has been paid off already, that we occupy a high position in the eyes of the world, and that we are fast coming back to our old prosperity. Accuse the opposition of endeavoring to cut down the duties on imports, and so bring the pauper labor of Europe in competition with that of our industrious mechanics; denounce them as sympathisers with rebellion; accuse them of attempting to revive dead issues, and to unsettle questions that had been disposed of by war, and the logic of accepted facts. If a Democrat you show that the administration is unnecessarily and enormously expensive; that extravagance and corruption mark every step of the government; that the men in power keep the war in the South alive long after peace has been declared; accuse them of revenue schemes to make the rich richer and the poor, poorer; and hold them as the party in power responsible for all the wrong of legislation, and all the fraud in the executive offices.

But, if you are a novice, you will not cover so much ground, and you will do what little you do, in a more artistic way. Take up any one of the subjects named, but prepare for it first by some reference to the aim and object of government—the reasons why men enter into communities, and submit to rules; the principles that should govern the action of departments of the public service. Then show where and how the particular action of the opposite side which you select for attack, violates these principles, and conflicts with those aims and objects; and ask your auditors to stamp their disapproval on the action of the other party by the only practical way they can do it, namely, by voting for your side; for your principles and for the men who are pledged to maintain them.

But above all, be brief, a political speech over twenty minutes long is a nuisance, which should subject its perpetrator to the horse-pond. There is an exception to this. If you are the only speaker, and it is a country place where the audience has come from great distances, and has nothing to occupy it, and looks to be made up of patient people—then you may make a long speech, about a half hour. And don't warn people that you are about to close, so that some one may cry "go on," by way of compliment, though hoping you won't. Don't tell any one you are about to close, but close when you have done, without warning, or without that lingering and hesitation which a man feels who is about to be hanged. The essence of successful eloquence is made up of three things,—to have something to say; to say that something well; and to stop when you have said it.

In political speaking, as in nearly all speaking, a colloquial manner is best. The tone of voice should be that of ordinary earnest conversation. But with the occasion, the speaker will depart from this for a time. As he becomes excited he may even declaim; but he should be careful to avoid rant. The human vocal organs form an instrument upon which a man must play, and he will play better by practice; but he must endeavor to keep full control of the instrument. But of that we will have more to say in another place.

It is not alone in the ward meeting, or the district public assembly that political speeches are delivered. In caucuses or conventions, which are the legislatures of the political parties, a number of subjects come up for discussion; party action is shaped ; and principles of action, as well as action itself, are determined. The speaking here is of a different character, and is much easier than the set speech. In a debate opposite views are brought out, and the excitement of opposition *develops* ideas, and aids expression. A man may labor in a set speech, and labor to little purpose, who will figure quite *effectively* in debate. Even the set speech which often is given in a party convention, partakes of the argumentative rather than the declamatroy character. In some parts of the country political meetings are got up for debate. Both sides are represented on the stump, and the result is that the auditors learn something. Where a meeting is entirely in the interest of one party, speakers are apt to be loose in their statements, and to deal extravagantly with facts. But where a speaker knows he is to be followed by some one who will attempt to refute his positions, he is careful in his statements, and makes his side as strong as possible by stating no more than he can maintain.

Never underrate the capacity of your audience. There are no better judges of speaking than your unlettered men ; because they hear so much of it, and often by men of mark, and because your unlettered man may have as much brains as the learned, though under less culture. And though the speaker who indulges in buffoonery, or who uses fine rhetorical figures, is often applauded to the echo, you will find that the man who takes a plain, common sense view of his subject, who states his case plainly and precisely, who wastes no words, and who brings to his task knowledge, earnestness and simplicity of diction, will be listened to with intense attention, and will command the respect which the more flashy and humorous orator will fail to win.

We do not wish to denounce either humor, or the proper use of fine figures of speech. But both these are mere accessories. They should not make the staple of the oration. And humor is a very dangerous edged tool, that is apt to cut the hands of the unskillful workman. It is quite rare that it can be carried to any great extent, with any profit. We know of few instances to the contrary, but those are quite remarkable ; and these were in legislative assemblages, and will be noticed elsewhere. A quite suc-

cessful instance is in the following, which is part of a speech
delivered before a Democratic convention by Thomas Dunn
English, in July, 1860, as we find it reported in a Trenton
journal of that time :

" After the very spirit-stirring appeal made by the gentleman who has
preceded me (Mr. Maar), I fear that what I may say will only tend to
pale the enthusiasm which he has generated—an enthusiasm which
reminds me of the fiery days of the party, even as I am old enough to
remember it. And I am placed in a more unfortunate position than
that gentleman, because I have not even a refuge in that embarrassment of which he speaks—(Laughter.) I have very little, if any,
modesty to fall back upon. In my early days—my time of juvenile
innocence—I possessed modesty to an alarming extent, no doubt ; but
as I rose to manhood it wore away ;—time rubbed the down off the
peach, and left me perfectly able to take care of myself on all occasions.
I am not at all embarrassed at appearing before a mass of Democrats
anywhere, and feel perfectly willing, on all proper occasions, to avow
my views and sentiments. Nor am I discouraged by the circumstances
amid which we stand to-day. I am not alarmed for the future of
the Democratic party, because some who were so long with us—men
who have led us in many a fight—have gone after strange gods, and
deserted, in their man worsship, the trusts they held. The leaders of
the Democratic party are not its masters, but its executive officers.
(Cheers.) If they fail or falter. we depose them, and choose their
successors from the ranks. (Cheers) · The path of progress of the
Democratic party is strewn with the carcasses of leaders—of men
whose names were our watchwords, but who placed themselves in the
road of its march to stay or swerve it, and so they perished. The
policy of the party is based upon the necessities of. the country. It
applies eternal and unchanging principles to those necessities ; and so
its policy grows, shifts or changes, with the progress of the Nation,
but the principles never change.

" If they be lost sight of for a brief time, as in the case of the resolu-
tions of 1798, they are sure to reassert themselves and regain their old
force. Our policy is based upon the true principles, and preserves the
Union by adhering to the letter of the Constitution and preserving the
equality of the states. We guarantee and defend the rights of each
part and portion of the confederacy. To-day one section is assailed
and we sustain it, not to please that section, but because our course
is right. We cannot afford—least of all the citizens of New Jersey—
to see the rights of any member of our confederacy invaded. Here
we are, citizens of this plucky little state, placed between the two
leading states for population, power and wealth, in all the Union.
We have no armed forces, no natural defense, no mountain fastnesses,
and we are but few in number. Yet who doubts if we were assailed,
that the manly hearts of our people would impel their strong arms to
fight in defence of their reserved rights—to fight to the last man and
the last drop of blood. Do we think that there is any state in the

South who would do less! If so we should put it out of the Union speedily as too degraded to be our peer. And it is to mete to other states what we demand—to maintain their perfect equality with us — that we are prepared and willing to contend for their rights. It is our own battles we fight. We do right not to please a section, but because it is right of itself. (Cheers.) And if leaders, to pander to the morbid sentiment of fanaticism, violate the policy which has brought them into power and position, they will live to see their names, like those of others that once occupied a high place in the temple of the party, effaced so fully that they never may be restored. They will not find themselves necessary to our existence or our prosperity. We can replace them at our will.—The exigency of the moment will bring us leaders for a struggle, as it has brought them before. We have in our ranks, no doubt, though you and I may not see them at this moment, many men who are fit to take command. We are too apt to under-value the great men of our own time by contrasting them unfavorably with their predecessors—men who are scorned by their cotemporaries in the same way. The dwarfs of the present may become the giants of the future. (Cheers.) I do not much indulge in comparison, but I remember a fact, trifling in itself, which I once mentioned in a dinner-speech and which comes to my mind aptly. I was traveling, a few years since, on horseback, toward the close of a summer's day, in the Western part of a neighboring state. My path—it could scarcely be called a road—lay over a succession of mountain ridges. All day long I had witnessed the same scenery—the rough masses of rock, the grey earth, the dense undergrowth, and the tall trees, branchless from root to summit fork—all similar and all monotonous. I thought the scenery commonplace. I was wearied with the recurrence of tree and rock and shrub, as well as jaded with travel. When I reached the valley I turned accidentally, and glanced upward. There before me, towering in lofty majesty, was the mountain down whose sides I had ridden—the hues of leaf and soil and rock blending into each other, the rugged outlines softened down by the atmosphere and smoothed by the distance, and the summit crowned by the rays of the setting sun. Time is the distance which will smooth the ruggedness of the great men around us, wrap the body of their fame in aerial garments, and crown their brow with the sunset rays of a golden immortality. (Enthusiastic cheering.)"

In the light of later events parts of the speech seem like an echo from the grave; but still one can see in the general style, and in the metaphor at the close of the part we have extracted, how and why the audience were moved.

PART I-V.—OF LEGISLATIVE SPEAKING.

IN public legislative bodies, whether the town council, the state assembly or Congress, all debate is conducted by certain set rules, in order to preserve decorum, and facilitate the despatch of business. These rules, which are to be found in certain published "manuals," should be thoroughly learned by every member; as without that knowledge he will find his influence reduced to the smallest amount and his eloquence clogged by frequent unpleasant interruptions. In all such bodies time is of value, and every one who participates in discussion has no right to waste the time of others, however liberal he may be with his own.

In a debate, though no one should rise too often on the same subject, the main speech he may make will often be supplemented by others; and the interpolations of his antagonist will soon cause his oration to take the shape of a polylogue. But the rules governing the main speech are the same as in the dinner, or stump oration. It is to be constructed on the same principles.

In the first place the subject itself should be previously mastered in all its bearings, if the speaker be not well acquainted with it already. In the second place, he should state his views briefly and without attempts at ornament. Unless he means to speak but once, he should reserve sarcasm, humor and the use of striking figures of rhetoric for a later period, when he desires to refute some points of his opponents, or overwhelm them with ridicule.

The novice in speaking—and it is for such we write—will not gain much by a close perusal of the debates in Congress or the state legislatures. Indeed, if he survived the amount of dullness thus taken into the brain, he would find his own intellect permanently weakened by the dull stuff it had imbibed. Some men improve in speaking by practice. There are those, however, who grow worse every day; and being dull at the beginning end in becoming stupid. A careful study of the styles of orators of reputation will be of more service, and be far less tiresome.

And in connection with this, a portion of a debate in the convention of Virginia, on the adoption of the Federal constitution, will give the reader a fair idea of the manner, and when we consider that the two engaged in it were Patrick Henry and Edmund Randolph, also of the matter of a first class debate. Patrick Henry, it will be remembered, was opposed to the ratification on the part of Virginia, of the constitution of the United States, and Edmund Randolph took the opposite ground. The extracts we make, though too short to do justice to the arguments, are sufficient to show the style of the parties, and should be carefully studied:

In his first speech on the question, among other things, Mr. Henry said.

"This constitution is said to have beautiful features; but when I come to examine these features, sir, they appear to me horribly frightful. Among other deformities, it has an awful squinting; it squints toward monarchy: and does not this raise indignation in the breast of every true American? Your President may easily become king. Your Senate is so imperfectly constructed, that your dearest rights may be sacrificed by what may be a small minority; and a very small minority may continue forever unchangeably this government, although horridly defective. Where are your checks in this government? Your strongholds will be in the hands of your enemies. It is on a supposition that your American governors shall be honest, that all the good qualities of this government are founded; but its defective and imperfect construction puts it in their power to perpetrate the worst of mischiefs, should they be bad men. And, sir, would not all the world, from the eastern to the western hemisphere, blame our distracted folly in resting our rights upon the contingency of our rulers being good or bad? Show me that age and country where the rights and liberties of the people were placed on the sole chance of their rulers being good men, without a consequent loss of liberty. I say that the loss of that dearest privilege has ever followed, with absolute certainty, every such mad attempt. If your American chief be a man of ambition and abilities, how easy will it be for him to render himself absolute! The army is in his hands, and, if he be a man of address, it will be attached to him: and it will be the subject of long meditation with him to seize the first auspicious moment to accomplish his design. And, sir, will the American spirit solely relieve you when this happens? I would rather infinitely—and I am sure most of this convention are of the same opinion, have a king, lords, and commons, then a government so replete with such insupportable evils. If we make a king, we may prescribe the rules by which he shall rule his people, and interpose such checks as shall prevent him from infringing them; but the President in the field, at the head of his army, an pre

scribe the terms on which he shall reign master, so far that it will
puzzle any American ever to get his neck from under the galling yoke.
I cannot, with patience, think of this idea. If ever he violates the
laws, one of two things will happen; he will come at the head of his
army to carry everything before him; or, he will give bail, or do what
Mr. Chief Justice will order him. If he be guilty, will not the recol-
lection of his crimes teach him to make one bold push for the American
throne? Will not the immense difference between being master of
everything, and being ignominiously tried and punished, powerfully
excite him to make this bold push? But, sir, where is the existing
force to punish him? Can he not, at the head of his army beat down
every opposition? Away with your President; we shall have a king;
the army will salute him monarch; your militia will leave you, and
assist in making him king. and fight against you, and what have you to
oppose this force? What will then become of you and your rights?
Will not absolute despotism ensue?

*   *   *   *   *   *   *   *

" I trust, sir, the exclusion of the evils wherewith this system is
replete, in its present form, will be made a condition precedent to its
adoption, by this or any other state The transition from a general,
unqualified admission to offices, to a consolidation of government, seems
easy; for, though the American states are dissimilar in their structure,
this will assimilate them; this, sir, is itself a strong consolidating
feature, and is not one of the least dangerous in that system. Nine
states are insufficient to establish this government over those nine.
Imagine that nine have come into it. Virginia has certain scruples.
Suppose she will consequently refuse to join with those states; may
not they still continue in friendship and union with her? If she sends
her annual requisitions in dollars, do you think their stomachs will be
so squeamish as to refuse her dollars? Will they not accept her
regiments? They would intimidate you into an inconsiderate adoption,
and frighten you with ideal evils, and that the Union shall be dissolved.
'Tis a bug-bear, sir: the fact is, sir, that the eight adopting states can
hardly stand on their own legs. Public fame tells us, that the adopting states have already heart-burnings and animosity, and repent their
precipitate hurry: this, sir, may occasion exceeding great mischief.
When I reflect on these and many other circumstances, I must think
those states will be found to be in confederacy with us.

" If we pay our quota of money annually, and furnish our ratable
number of men, when necessary, I can see no danger from a rejection.
The history of Switzerland clearly proves, that we might be in amica-
ble alliance with those states, without adopting this Constitution.
Switzerland is a confederacy, consisting of dissimilar governments.
This is an example, which proves that governments, of dissimilar
structures, may be confederated. That confederate republic has stood
upward of four hundred years; and, although several of the individual
republics are democratic, and the rest aristocratic, no evil has resulted
from this dissimilarity, for they have braved all the power of France
and Germany, during that long period. The Swiss spirit, sir, has kept
them together; they have encountered and overcome immense diffi-

culties, with patience and fortitude In the vicinity of powerful and ambitious monarchs, they have retained their independence, republican simplicity and valor. Look at the peasants of that country, and of France, and mark the difference. You will find the condition of the former far more desirable and comfortable. No matter whether a people be great, splendid, and powerful, if they enjoy freedom. The Turkish Grand Seignior, alongside of our President, would put us to disgrace, but we should be abundantly consoled for this disgrace, should our citizen be put in contrast with the Turkish slave."

Mr. Randolph replied to this on the following day. From his speech we take the following passages :

"Instead of entering largely into a discussion of the nature and effect of the different kinds of government, or into an inquiry into the particular extent of country, that may suit the genius of this or that government, I ask this question—Is this government necessary for the safety of Virginia ? Is the union indispensable for our happiness ? I confess it is imprudent for any nation to form alliance with another, whose situation and construction of government are dissimilar with its own. It is impolitic and improper for men of opulence to join their interest with men of indigence and chance. But we are now inquiring, particularly, whether Virginia, as contradistinguished from the other states, can exist without the Union—a hard question, perhaps, after what has been said. I will venture, however, to say, she cannot. I shall not rest contented with asserting—I shall endeavor to prove. Look at the most powerful nations on earth. England and France have had recourse to this expedient. Those countries found it necessary to unite with their immediate neighbors, and this union has prevented the most lamentable mischiefs.

"What divine preëminence is Virginia possessed of, above other states ? Can Virginia send her navy and thunder, to bid defiance to foreign nations ? And can she exist without a union with her neighbors, when the most potent nations have found such a union necessary, not only to their political felicity, but their national existence ? Let us examine her ability. Although it be impossible to determine, with accuracy, what degree of internal strength a nation ought to possess, to enable it to stand by itself ; yet there are certain sure facts and circumstances, which demonstrate, that a particular nation cannot stand singly. I have spoken with freedom, and I trust I have done it with decency ; but I must also speak with truth. If Virginia can exist without the union, she must derive that ability from one or other of these sources, viz: from her natural situation, or because she has no reason to fear from other nations. What is her situation ? She is not inaccessible. She is not a petty republic, like that of St. Marino, surrounded with rocks and mountains, with a soil not very fertile, nor worthy the envy of surrounding nations. Were this, sir, her situation, she might, like that petty state, subsist separated from all the world. On the contrary she is very accessible ; the large, capacious bay of Chesapeake, which is but too excellently adapted for the admission of enemies, renders her very vulnerable. I am informed, and I believe rightly, because I derive my information from those whose knowledge is most respectable, that Virginia is in a very unhappy position, with repect to the access of foes by sea, though happily situated for commerce. This being her situation by sea, let us look at land. She has frontiers adjoining the states of Pennsylvania, Maryland and North Carolina. Two of these states have declared themselves members of the Union. Will she be inaccessible to the inhabitants of those states? Cast your eyes to the western country, that is inhabited by cruel savages, your natural enemies. Besides their natural propensity to barbarity, they may be excited, by the gold of foreign enemies, to commit the most horrid ravages on your people. Our great, increasing population is one remedy to this evil; but, being scattered thinly over so extensive a country, how difficult is it to collect their strength, or defend the country.

" If then, sir, Virginia, from her situation, is not inaccessible, or invulnerable, let us consider if she be protected, by having no cause to fear from other nations: has she no cause to fear? You will have cause to fear as a nation, if disunited; you will not only have this cause to fear from yourselves, from that species of population I before mentioned, and your once sister states, but from the arms of other nations. Have you no cause of fear from Spain, whose dominions border on your country? Every nation, every people, in our circumstances, have always had abundant cause to fear. Let us see the danger to be apprehended from France; let us suppose Virginia separated from the other states: as part of the former confederated states, she will owe France a very considerable sum—France will be as magnanimous as ever. France, by the law of nations, will have a right to demand the whole of her, or of the others. If France were to demand it, what would become of the property of America? Could she not destroy what little commerce we have? Could she not seize our ships, and carry havoc and destruction before her on our shores? The most lamentable desolation would take place. We owe a debt to Spain also; do we expect indulgence from that quarter? That nation has a right to demand the debt due to it, and power to enforce that right. Will the Dutch be silent about the debt due to them? Is there any one pretension, that any of these nations will be patient? The debts due the British also very considerable: these debts have been withheld contrary to treaty; if Great Britain will demand the payment of these debts, peremptorily, what will be the consequence? Can we pay them if demanded? Will no danger result from a refusal? Will the British nation suffer their subjects to be stripped of their property? Is not that nation amply able to do its subjects justice? Will the resentment of that powerful and supercilious nation sleep forever? If we become one, sole nation, uniting with our sister states, our means of defence will be greater; the indulgence for the payment of those debts will be greater, and the danger of an attack less probable. Moreover, vast quantities of lands have been sold, by citizens of this country, to Europeans, and these lands cannot be found. Will this fraud be countenanced or endured? Among so many causes of danger, shall we be secure, separated from our sister states? Weakness itself, sir, will invite some attack upon your country. Contemplate our situation deliberately, and consult history : it will inform you, that people in our circumstances have ever been attacked, and successfully : open any page, and you will there find our danger truly depicted. If such a people had any thing, was it not taken? The fate which will befall us. I fear, sir, will be, that we shall be made a partition of. How will these our troubles be removed? Can we have any dependence on commerce? Can we make any computation on this subject? Where will our flag appear? So high is the spirit of commercial nations, that they will spend five times the value of the object, to exclude their rivals from a participation in commercial profits ; they seldom regard any expenses. If we should be divided from the rest of the states, upon what footing would our navigation in the Mississippi be? What would be the probable conduct of France and Spain?

"I will close this catalogue of the evils of the dissolution of the Union, by recalling to your mind what passed in the year 1781. Such was the situation of our affairs then, that the powers of a dictator were given to the commander-in-chief to save us from destruction. This shows the situation of the country to have been such as made it ready to embrace an actual dictator. At some future period, will not our distresses impel us to do what the Dutch have done—throw all power into the hands of a stadtholder? How infinitely more wise and eligible, than this desperate alternative, is a union with our American brethren! I feel myself so abhorrent to any thing that will dissolve our Union, that I cannot prevail with myself to assent to it directly or indirectly. If the union is to be dissolved, what step is to be taken? Shall we form a partial confederacy ; or is it expected that we shall successfully apply to foreign alliance for military aid? This last measure, sir, has ruined almost every nation that has used it ; so dreadful an example ought to be most cautiously avoided ; for seldom has a nation recurred to the expedient of foreign succor without being ultimately crushed by that succor. We may lose our liberty and independence by this injudicious scheme of policy. Admitting it to be a scheme replete with safety, what nation shall we solicit—France? She will disdain a connection with a people in our predicament. I would trust every thing to the magnanimity of that nation ; but she would despise a people who had, like us, so imprudently separated from their brethren ; and, sir, were she to accede to our proposal, with what facility could she become mistress of our country! To what nation then shall we apply—to Great Britain? Nobody has as yet trusted that idea. An application to any other must be either fruitless or dangerous ; to those who advocate local confederacies, and at the same time preach up for republican liberty, I answer, that their conduct is inconsistent ; the defense of such partial confederacies will require such a degree of force and expense as will destroy every feature of republicanism. Give me leave to say, that I see naught but destruction in a local confederacy. With what state can we confederate but North Carolina—North Carolina, situated worse than ourselves? Consult your own reason? I beseech gentlemen most

seriously to reflect on the consequences of such a confederacy; I beseech them to consider whether Virginia and North Carolina, both
oppressed with debts and slaves, can defend themselves externally, or
make their people happy internally.   North Carolina having no strength
but militia. and Virginia in the same situation, will make, I fear, but
a despicable figure in history.   Thus, sir, I hope that I have satisfied
you that we are unsafe without a union, and that in union alone safety
consists.

"But the amendability of the confederation seems to have great
weight on the minds of some gentlemen.   To what point will the
amendments go ?   What part makes the most important figure ?
What part deserves to be retained ?   In it, one body has the legislative, executive and judicial powers; but the want of efficient powers
has prevented the dangers naturally consequent on the union of these.
Is this union consistent with an augmentation of their power ?   Will
you then amend it, by taking away one of these three powers ?   Suppose, for instance, you only vested it with the legislative and executive
powers, without any control on the judiciary, what must be the result ?
Are we not taught by reason, experience and governmental history,
that tyranny is the natural and certain consequence of uniting these
two powers, or the legislative and judicial powers exclusively, in the
same body ?   If any one denies it, I shall pass by him as an infidel not
to be reclaimed.   Wherever any two of these three powers are vested
in one single body, they must, at one time or other, terminate in the
destruction of liberty.   In the most important cases, the assent of nine
states is necessary to pass a law; this is too great a restriction. and
whatever good consequences it may in some cases produce, yet it will
prevent energy in many other cases; it will prevent energy, which is
most necessary on some emergencies, even in cases wherein the existence of the community depends on vigor and expedition.   It is incom-
patible with that secrecy which is the life of execution and despatch.
Did ever thirty or forty men retain a secret ?   Without secrecy no
government can carry on its operations on great occasions; this is
what gives that superiority in action to the government of one.   If any
thing were wanting to complete this farce, it would be that a resolution
of the assembly of Virginia and the other legislatures, should be
necessary to confirm and render of any validity the congressional acts;
this would openly discover the debility of the general government to
all the world.   But, in fact, its imbecility is now nearly the same as if
such acts were formally requisite.   An act of the assembly of Virginia,
controverting a resolution of congress, would certainly prevail.   I
therefore conclude that the confederation is too defective to deserve
correction.   Let us take farewell of it with reverential respect, as an
old benefactor.   It is gone, whether this house says so or not.   It is
gone, sir, by its own weakness.

"I have labored for the continuance of the Union—the rock of our
salvation.   I believe that as sure as there is a God in heaven, our
safety, our political happiness and existence, depend on the union of
the states; and that, without this union, the people of this and the
other states will undergo the unspeakable calamities which discord,

factioa, turbulence, war and bloodshed have produced in other countries. The American spirit ought to be mixed with American pride—pride to see the union magnificently triumph. Let that glorious pride which once defied the British thunder, reanimate you again. Let it not be recorded of Americans, that, after having performed the most gallant exploits, after having overcome the most astonishing difficulties, and after having gained the admiration of the world--by their incomparable valor and policy, they lost their acquired reputation, their national consequence and happiness, by their own indiscretion. Let no future historian inform posterity that they wanted wisdom and virtue to concur in any regular, efficient government. Should any writer, doomed to so disagreeable a task, feel the indignation of an honest historian, he would reprehend and recriminate our folly with equal severity and justice. Catch the present moment; seize it with avidity and eagerness; for it may be lost, never to be regained. If the Union be now lost, I fear it will remain so forever. I believe gentlemen are sincere in their opposition, and actuated by pure motives; but when I maturely weigh the advantages of the Union, and dreadful consequences of its dissolution; when I see safety on my right, and destruction on my left; when I behold respectability and happiness acquired by the one, but annihilated by the other,—I cannot hesitate to decide in favor of the former."

From the three subsequent speeches of Mr. Henry in reply, we take the following:

"Switzerland consists of thirteen cantons expressly confederated for national defense. They have stood the shock of four hundred years; that country has enjoyed internal tranquillity most of that long period. Their dissensions have been, comparatively to those of other countries, very few. What has passed in the neighboring countries? Wars, dissensions, and intrigues—Germany involved in the most deplorable civil war thirty years successively, continually convulsed with intestine divisions, and harassed by foreign wars—France with her mighty monarchy perpetually at war. Compare the peasants of Switzerland with those of any other mighty nation: you will find them far more happy; for one civil war among them, there have been five or six among other nations; their attachment to their country, and to freedom, their resolute intrepidity in their defense, the consequent security and happiness which they have enjoyed, and the respect and awe which these things produced in their bordering nations, have signalized those republicans Their valor, sir, has been active; every thing that sets in motion the springs of the human heart, engaged them to the protection of their inestimable privileges. They have not only secured their own liberty, but have been the arbiters of the fate of other people. Here, sir, contemplate the triumph of republican governments over the pride of monarchy. I acknowledge, sir, that the necessity of national defence has prevailed in invigorating their counsels and arms, and has been, in a considerable degree, the means of keeping these honest people together. But, sir, they have had wisdom enough to keep together and render themselves formidable.

Their heroism is proverbial. They would heroically fight for their government and their laws. One of the illumined sons of these times would not fight for those objects. Those virtuous and simple people have not a mighty and splendid president, nor enormously expensive navies and armies to support No, sir; those brave republicans have acquired there reputation no less by their undaunted intrepidity, than by the wisdom of their frugal and economical policy. Let us follow their example, and be equally happy. The honorable member advises us to adopt a measure which will destroy our bill of rights; for, after hearing his picture of nations, and his reasons for abandoning all the powers retained to the States by the confederation I am more firmly persuaded of the impropriety of adopting this new plan in its present shape.

* * * * * * * *

" We are threatened with danger for the non-payment of the debt now due to France. We have information from an illustrious citizen of Virginia, who is now in Paris, which disproves the suggestions of such danger. This citizen has not been in the airy regions of theoretic speculation: our ambassador is this worthy citizen. The ambassador of the United States of America is not so despised as the honorable gentleman would make us believe. A servant of a republic is as much respected as that of a monarch. The honorable gentleman tells us that hostile fleets are to be sent to make reprisals upon us: our ambassador tells you that the king of France has taken into consideration, to enter into commercial regulations on reciprocal terms with us. which will be of peculiar advantage to us. Does this look like hostility? I might go further; I might say, not from public authority, but good information, that his opinion is, that you reject this government. His character and abilities are in the highest estimation; he is well acquainted, in every respect, with this country; equally so with the policy of the European nations. This illustrious citizen advises you to reject this government, till it be amended. His sentiments coincide entirely with ours. His attachment to, and services done for, this country are well known. At a great distance from us, he remembers and studies our happiness. Living amidst splendor and dissipation, he thinks yet of bills of rights—thinks of those little despised things called maxims Let us follow the sage advice of this common friend of our happiness. It is little usual for nations to send armies to collect debts The house of Bourbon. that great friend of America, will never attack her for the unwilling delay of payment. Give me leave to say that Europe is too much engaged about objects of greater importance to attend to us. On that great theater of the world, the little American matters vanish. Do you believe that the mighty monarch of France. beholding the greatest scenes that ever engaged the attention of a prince of that country, will divert himself from those important objects, and now call for a settlement of accounts with America? This proceeding is not warranted by good sense. The friendly disposition to us, and the actual situation of France, render the idea of danger from that quarter absurd. Would this countryman of ours be fond of advising us to a measure which he knew to be dangerous—and can it be reasonably supposed, that he can be ignorant of any premeditated hostility against this country? The honorable gentleman may suspect the account: but I will do our friend the justice to say that he would warn us of any danger from France.

" Do you suppose the Spanish monarch will risk a contest with the United States, when his feeble colonies are exposed to them? Every advance the people here make to the westward, makes him tremble for Mexico and Peru. Despised as we are among ourselves under our present government, we are terrible to that monarchy. If this be not a fact, it is generally said so.

* * * * * * * *

"This government is so new that it wants a name. I wish its other novelties were as harmless as this. He told us we had an American dictator in the year 1781. We never had an American President. In making a dictator we followed the example of the most glorious, magnanimous, and skillful nations. In great dangers this power has been given. Rome had furnished us with an illustrious example. America found a person worthy of that trust; she looked to Virginia for him. We gave a dictatorial power to hands that used it gloriously and which were rendered more glorious by surrendering it up. Where is there a breed of such dictators? Shall we find a set of American Presidents of such a breed? Will the American President come and lay prostrate at the feet of Congress his laurels? I fear there are few men who can be trusted on that head. The glorious republic of Holland, has erected monuments to her warlike intrepidity and valor ; yet she is now totally ruined by a stadtholder, a Dutch president. The destructive wars into which that nation has been plunged have since involved her in ambition. The glorious triumphs of Blenheim and Ramillies were not so conformable to the genius, nor so much to the true interest of the republic, as those numerous and useful canals and dikes, and other objects at which ambition spurns. That republic has, however, by the industry of its inhabitants and policy of its magistrates, suppressed the ill effects of ambition. Notwithstanding two of their provinces have paid nothing, yet I hope the example of Holland will tell us that we can live happily without changing our present despised government. Cannot people be as happy under a mild as under an energetic government? Cannot content and felicity be enjoyed in a republic as well as in a monarchy, because there are whips, chains, and scourges used in the latter? If I am not as rich as my neighbor, if I give my mite, my all, republican forbearance will say that it is sufficient. So said the honest confederates of Holland ; 'You are poor ; we are rich. We will go on and do better, far better, than be under an oppressive government.' Far better will it be for us to continue as we are, than go under that tight, energetic government. I am persuaded of what the honorable gentleman says, that separate confederacies will ruin us. In my judgment, they are evils never to be thought of till a people are driven by necessity. When he asks my opinion of consolidation, of one power to reign over America with a strong hand, I will tell him, I am persuaded of the rectitude of my honorable friend's opinion (Mr. Mason), that one government cannot reign over so extensive a country as this is, without absolute despotism. Compared to such a consolidation, small confederacies are little evils, though they ought to be recurred to but in case of necessity. Virginia and North Carolina are despised. They could exist separated from the rest of America. Maryland and Vermont were not overrun when out of the confederacy. Though it is not a desirable object, yet. I trust, that on examination it will be found, that Virginia and North Carolina would not be swallowed up in case it was necessary for them to be joined together.

*　　*　　*　　*　　*　　*　　*　　*

" I call upon every gentleman here to declare, whether the king of England had any subjects so attached to his family and government— so loyal as we were. But the genius of Virginia called us for liberty; called us from those beloved endearments, which, from long habits, we were taught to love and revere. We entertained from our earliest infan·y the most sincere regard and reverence for the mother coun- try. Our partiality extended to a predilection for her customs, habits, manners, and laws. Thus inclined, when the deprivation of our lib- erty was attempted, what did we do? What did the genius of Virginia tell us? 'Sell all and purchase liberty.' This is a .severe conflict. Republican maxims were then esteemed. Those maxims and the genius of Virginia landed you safe on the shore of freedom. On this awful occasion, did you want a federal government? Did federal ideas possess your minds? Did federal ideas lead you to the most splendid victories? I must again repeat the favorite idea, that the genius of Virginia did, and will again lead us to happiness. To obtain the most splendid prize, you did not consolidate. You accomplished the most glorious ends by the assistance of the genius of your country. Men were then taught by that genius that they were fighting for what was most dear to them. View the most affectionate father. the most tender mother, operated on by liberty, nobly stimulating their sons, their dearest sons, sometimes their only son, to advance to the defense of his country. We have seen sons of Cincinnatus, without splendid magnificence or parade, going, with the genius of their progenitor Cincinnatus to the plow—men who served their country without ruining it; men who had served it to the destruction of their private patrimonies ; their country owing them amazing amounts, for the pay- ment of which no adequate provision was then made. We have seen such men throw prostrate their arms at your feet. ·They did not call for those emoluments which ambition presents to some imaginations The soldiers who were able to command every thing, instead of tram- pling on those laws which they were instituted to defend, most strictly obeyed them. The hands of justice have not been laid on a single American soldier. Bring them into contrast with European veterans —you will see an astonishing superiority over the latter. There has been a strict subordination to the laws. The honorable gentleman's office gave him an opportunity of viewing if the laws were administered so as to prevent riots, routs, and unlawful assemblies From his then situation. he could have furnished us with the instances in which licentiousness trampled on the laws.

" Among all our troubles, we have paid almost to the last shilling, for the sake of justice ; we have paid as well as any state ; I will not say better. To support the general government and our own legislature ; to pay the interest of the public debts, and defray contingencies, we have been heavily taxed. To add to these things, the distresses produced by paper money, and by tobacco contracts, were sufficient to render any people discontented. These, sir, were great temptations ; but in the most severe conflict of misfortunes, this code of laws—this genius of Virginia, call it what you will, triumphed ever everything.

*   *   *   *   *   *   *   *

" I am constrained to make a few remarks on the absurdity of adopting this system, and relying on the chance of getting it amended afterward. When it is confessed to be replete with defects, is it not offering to insult your understandings, to attempt to reason you out of the propriety of rejecting it, till it be amended ? Does it not insult your judgments to tell you—adopt first, and then amend ? Is your rage for novelty so great, that you are first to sign and seal, and then to retract ? Is it possible to conceive a greater solecism ? I am at a loss what to say. You agree to bind yourselves hand and foot—for the sake of what ? Of being unbound. You go into a dungeon—for what ? To get out. Is there no danger, when you go in, that the bolts of federal authority shall shut you in ? Human nature never will part from power. Look for an example of a voluntary relinquishment of power, from one end of the globe to another—you will find none. Nine-tenths of our fellow-men have been, and are now, depressed by the most intolerable slavery, in the different parts of the world ; because the strong hand of power has bolted them in the dungeon of despotism. Review the present situation of the nations of Europe, which is pretended to be the freest quarter of the globe. Cast your eyes on the countries called free there. Look at the country from which we are descended, I beseech you ; and although we are separated by everlasting, insuperable partitions, yet there are some virtuous people there who are friends to human nature and liberty. Look at Britain ; see there the bolts and bars of power ; see bribery and corruption defiling the fairest fabric that ever human nature reared. Can a gentleman who is an Englishman, or who is acquainted with the English history desire to prove these evils ? See the efforts of a man descended from a friend of America : see the efforts of that man, assisted even by the king, to make reforms. But you find the faults too strong to be amended. Nothing but bloody war can alter them. See Ireland : that country groaned from century to century, without getting their government amended. Previous adoption was the fashion there. They sent for amendments from time to time, but never obtained them, though pressed by the severest oppression, till eighty thousand volunteers demanded them sword in hand—till the power of Britain was prostrate ; when the American resistance was crowned with success. Shall we do so ? If you judge by the experience of Ireland, you must obtain the amendments as early as possible. But I ask you again, where is the example that a government was amended by those who instituted it ? Where is the instance of the errors of a government rectified by those who adopted them ?

*   *   *   *   *   *   *   *

"' Perhaps I shall be told, that I have gone through the regions of
fancy; that I deal in noisy exclamations and mighty professions of
patriotism. Gentlemen may retain their opinions; but I look on that
paper as the most fatal plan that could possibly be conceived to enslave
a free people. If such be your rage for novelty, take it and welcome; ·
but you never shall have my consent. My sentiments may appear extravagant, but I can tell you, that a number of my fellow-citizens have
kindred sentiments ; and I am anxious, if my country should come into
the hands of tyranny, to exculpate myself from being in any degree the
cause, and to exert my faculties to the utmost to extricate her.
Whether I am gratified or not in my beloved form of government, I
consider that the more she is plunged into distress, the more it is my
duty to relieve her. Whatever may be the result, I shall wait with
patience till the day may come when an opportunity shall offer to exert
myself in her cause.

"But I should be led to take that man for a lunatic, who should tell
me to run into the adoption of a government avowedly defective, in
hopes of having it amended afterward. Were I about to give away
the meanest particle of my own property, I should act with more
prudence and discretion. My anxiety and fears are great, lest
America, by the adoption of this system, should be cast into a fathom-
less abyss."

Without the whole speeches—and these, lack of space
forbids us to give—the reader loses the nice points on both
sides; but he readily perceives the great secret of the effect
of the debate, which is the secret of the effect of eloquence
always—namely, earnestness. The speakers believe what
they say and are endeavoring to impress others with that
belief. And this earnestness is called out more strongly
by the opposition. Each is master of his subject; each is
earnest in its support; and each uses simple and appropriate
language to express his opinions. In fact, we know of
nothing better as a foundation of style in speaking—not
even the speeches of Demosthenes in the original, than a
close study of the debates, poorly as they are reported,
of the convention that framed the United States Constitution, or that of any of the states who met to consider the
propriety of ratifying it. For to such bodies, in those days,
they sent men of brains and culture, and those took their
legitimate lead.

Of course, if the reader of this little work, ever goes to
a constitutional convention, or Congress, he will not need,
or will not think he needs any hints from us. It is the

heaven-inspired privilege of your congressman or legislator
to know everything, though, with an astonishing stinginess;
he keeps that knowledge generally pretty closely to himself. But to the novice, before he gets to Congress, our
instruction may be of some use, and hence we have devoted
so much of our space to general principles, and to extracts
in illustration

We have previously spoken of humor, and how dangerous it is in unpracticed hands. With the skilled speaker it
becomes a powerful weapon. Two instances in our congressional history occur to us, where the use of sarcasm—
for it is this form of humor which is most forcible in debate
—had astonishing effect. The first was by the late Thomas
Corwin. It was in Congress in 1840. Mr. Crary, of
Michigan, in a speech on some particular subject, made a
fierce attack upon General Harrison, who was a candidate
for the presidency at the time; and in a labored speech
endeavored to show that General Harrison was very incom-
petent as a military man, and had blundered terribly at the
battle of Tippecanoe. Thereupon Corwin replied in an
admirable bantering speech, whose irony was so severe that
it not only closed Crary's mouth for the time, but drove
him from public life altogether. The second is more recent. There is a bill which proposes to grant a certain
amount of public land for the St. Croix railroad—or rather
it is proposed to renew the grant in a former bill, which
failed to be used in time. The bill has been rejected, but
returns again. Last year it made its appearance. Mr. J.
Proctor Knott, of Kentucky, was not satisfied with the bill,
but did not care to argue seriously upon what he supposed
to be a mere attempt to get more of the public domain away
from its owners. After speaking in a humorous way con-
cerning the St. Croix region, and holding up the friends of
the measure and the measure itself to ridicule, he turned to
the town of Minnesota which was to be chiefly benefited by
the measure, and paid his respects to it, in the following
style :

"Now, sir, I repeat I have been satisfied for years that if there was
any portion of the inhabited globe absolutely in a suffering condition
for want of a railroad, it was these teeming pine barrens of St. Croix.

(Laughter.) At what particular point on that noble stream such a road should be commenced I know was immaterial, and so it seems to have been considered by the draughtsman of this bill. It might be up at the spring or down at the foot-log, or the water-gate, or the fish-dam. or anywhere along the bank, no matter where. (Laughter.) But in what direction it should run, or where it should terminate. were always to my mind questions of the most painful perplexity. I could conceive of no place on 'God's green earth' in such straightened circumstances for railroad facilities as to be likely to desire or willing to accept such a connection. (Laughter.) I know that neither Bayfield nor Superior City would have it, for they both indignantly spurned the munificence of the government when coupled with such ignominious conditions, and let this very same land grant die on their hands years and years ago, rather than submit to the degradation of direct communication by railroad with the piney woods of the St. Croix; and I know that what the enterprising inhabitants of those giant young cities would refuse to take would have few charms for others, whatever their necessities or cupidity might be. (Laughter.) Hence, as I have said, sir, I was utterly at a loss to determine where the terminus of this great and indispensable road should be, until I accidentally overheard some gentlemen the other day mention the name of "Duluth.' (Great laughter.) Duluth. The word fell upon my ear with peculiar and indescribable charm, like the gentle murmur of a low fountain stealing forth in the midst of roses, or the soft sweet accents of an angel's whisper in the bright, joyous dream of sleeping innocence.

"Duluth! 'Twas the name for which my soul had panted for years, as the hart panteth for the water-brooks! (Renewed laughter) But where was Duluth? Never, in all my limited reading, had my vision been gladdened by seeing thecelestial word in print. (Laughter.) And I felt a profounder humiliation in my ignorance that its dulcet syllables had never before ravished my delighted ear. (Roars of laughter.) I was certain the draughtsman of this bill had never heard of it, or it would have been designated as one of the termini of this road. I asked my friends about it, but they knew nothing of it I rushed to the library and examined all the maps I could find. (Laughter.) I discovered in one of them a delicate, hair-like line, diverging from the Mississippi near a place called Prescott, which I suppose was intended to represent the river St. Croix, but I could nowhere find Duluth !

"Nevertheless, I was confident that it existed somewhere, and that its discovery would constitute the crowning glory of the present century, if not of all modern times. (Laughter.) I knew it was bound to exist in the very nature of things; that the symmetry and perfection of our planetary system would be incomplete without it, (renewed laughter) ; that the elements of material nature would long since have resolved themselves back into original chaos if there had been such a hiatus in creation as would have resulted from leaving out Duluth (Roars of laughter.) In fact, sir. I was overwhelmed with the conviction that Duluth not only existed somewhere, but that, wherever it was, it was a great and glorious place. I was convinced that the greatest calamity that ever befell the benighted nations of the ancient world was in their having passed away without a knowledge of the actual existence of Duluth; that their fabled Atlantis, never seen save by the hallowed vision of inspired poesy, was, in fact, but another name for Duluth; that the golden orchard of the Hesperides was but a poetical synonym for the beer gardens in the vicinity of Duluth. (Great laughter.) I was certain that Herodotus had died a miserable death. because in all his travels, and with all his geographical research, he had never heard of Duluth. (Laughter.) I knew that if the immortal spirit of Homer could look down from another heaven than that created by his own celestial genius, upon the long lines of pilgrims from every nation of the earth to the gushing fountain of poesy opened by the touch of his magic wand; if he could be permitted to behold the vast assemblage of grand and glorious productions of the lyric art called into being by his own inspired strains, he would weep tears of bitter anguish that, instead of lavishing all the stores of his mighty genius upon the fall of Ilion, it had not been his more blessed lot to crystalize in deathless song the rising glories of Duluth. (Great and continued laughter.) Yet, sir, had it not been for this map, kindly furnished me by the Legislature of Minnesota, I might have gone down to my obscure and humble grave in an agony of despair because I could nowhere find Duluth. (Renewed laughter.) Had such been my melancholy fate, I have no doubt but that, with the last feeble pulsation of my breaking heart, with the last faint exhalation of my fleeting breath, I should have whispered. 'Where is Duluth?' (Roars of laughter.) But, thanks be to the beneficence of that band of ministering angels who have their bright abodes in the far-off capital of Minnesota, just as the agony of my anxiety was about to culminate in the frenzy of despair, this blessed map was placed in my hands and as I unfolded it a resplendent scene of ineffable glory opened before me, such as I imagine burst upon the enraptured vision of the wandering peri through the opening gates of paradise. (Renewed laughter.) Then, there for the first time, my enchanted eyes rested upon the ravishing word 'Duluth.'

"This map, sir, is intended, as it appears from its title, to illustrate the position of Duluth in the United States; but if gentlemen will examine it, I think they will concur with me in the opinion that it is far too modest in its pretensions. It not only illustrates the position of Duluth in the United States, but exhibits its relations with all created things. It even goes further than this. It lifts the shadowy veil of futurity and affords us a view of the golden prospects of Duluth far along the dim vista of ages yet to come.

"If gentlemen will examine it they will find Duluth not only in the center of the map, but represented in the center of a series of concentric circles one hundred miles apart, and some of them as much as four thousand miles in diameter, embracing alike in their tremendous sweep the fragrant savannas of the sunlit South and the eternal solitudes of snow that mantle the ice-bound North. (Laughter.) How these circles were produced is perhaps one of those primordial mysteries that the most skillful paleologists will never be able to explain. (Renewed laughter.) But the fact is, sir, Duluth is preeminently a central place, for I have been told by gentlemen who have been so reckless of their personal safety as to venture away into those awful regions where Duluth is supposed to be, that it is so exactly in the center of the visible universe that the sky comes down at precisely the same distance all around it. (Roars of laughter.) I find by reference to this map that Duluth is situated somewhere near the western end of Lake Superior, but as there is no dot or other mark indicating its exact location, I am unable to say whether it is actually confined to any particular spot, or whether 'it is just lying around there loose.' (Renewed laughter.) I really cannot tell whether it is one of those ethereal creations of intellectual frost-work, more intangible than the rose tinted clouds of a summer sunset ; one of those airy exhalations of the speculator's brain which I am told are ever flitting in the form of towns and cities along the lines of railroad built with government subsidies, luring the unwary settler as the mirage of the desert lures the famishing traveler on, and ever on, until it fades away in the darkening horizon, or whether it is a real, *bona fide*, substantial city, all ' staked off,' with the lots marked with their owners' names like that proud commercial metropolis recently discovered on the desirable shores of San Domingo. (Laughter.) But, however that may be, I am satisfied Duluth is there, or there about, for I see it stated here on this map that it is exactly thirty-nine hundred and ninety miles from Liverpool (laughter), though I have no doubt for the sake of convenience, it will be moved back ten miles, so as to make the distance an even four thousand. (Renewed laughter.)

" Then, sir, there is the climate of Duluth, unquestionably the most salubrious and delightful to be found anywhere on the Lord's earth. Now, I have always been under the impression, as I presume other gentlemen have, that in the region around Lake Superior, it was cold enough for at least nine months in the year to freeze the smoke-stack off a locomotive. (Great laughter.) But I see it represented on this map that Duluth is situated exactly half way between the latitudes of Paris and Venice, so that gentlemen who have inhaled the exhilarating airs of the one, basked in the golden sunlight of the other may see at a glance that Duluth must be a place of untold delights (laughter), a terrestrial paradise fanned by the palmy zephyrs of an eternal spring, clothed in the gorgeous sheen of ever-blooming flowers, and vocal with the silver melody of nature's choicest songsters (Laughter) In fact, sir since I have seen this map I have no doubt that Byron was vainly endeavoring to convey some faint conceptions of the delicious charms of Duluth when his poetic soul gushed forth in the rippling strains of that beautiful rhapsody—

> Know ye the land of the cedar and pine,
> Where the flowers ever blossom, the beams ever shine ;
> Where the light wings of Zephyr. oppressed with perfume,
> Wax faint o'er the gardens of Gul in her bloom ;
> Where the citron and olive are fairest of fruit.
> And the voice of the nightingale never is mute ;
> Where the tints of the earth and the hues of the sky,
> In color, though varied, in beauty may vie ?

' As to the commercial resources. of Duluth, sir, they are simply illimitable, and inexhaustible, as is shown by this map. I see it stated here that there is a vast scope of territory, embracing an area of over ·,000,000 square miles, rich in every element of material wealth and commercial prosperity, all tributary to Duluth. Look at it, sir, (pointing to the map.) Here are inexhaustible mines of gold, immeasurable veins of silver, impenetrable depths of boundless forest, vast coal treasures, wide extended plains of richest pasturage, all, all embraced in this vast territory, which must, in the very nature of things, empty the untold treasures of its commerce into the lap of Duluth. (Laughter.) Look at it, sir, (pointing to the map); do not you see, from these broad, brown lines drawn around this immense territory, that the enterprising inhabitants of Duluth intend some day to inclose it all in one vast corral, so that its commerce will be bound to go there whether it would or not ? (Great laughter.) And here, sir (still pointing to the map), I find, within a convenient distance, the Piegan Indians, which, of all the many accessories to the glory of Duluth I consider by far the most estimable. For, sir, I have been told that when the small-pox breaks out among the women and children of that famous tribe, as it sometimes does, they afford the finest subject in the world for stragetical experiments, and any enterprising military hero who desires to improve himself in the noble art of war (laughter), especially for any lieutenant-general whose

> Trenchant blade Toledo trusty,
> For want of fighting has grown rusty,
> And eats into itself for lack
> Of somebody to hew and hack.

(Great laughter.)

" Sir, the great conflict now raging in the Old World has presented a phenomenon in military operations unprecedented in the annals of mankind, a phenomenon that has reversed all the traditions of the past as it has disappointed all the expectations of the present. A great and warlike people, renowned alike for their skill and valor, have been swept away before the triumphant advance of an inferior foe, like autumn stubble before a hurricane of fire. For aught I know, the next flash of electric fire that shimmers along the ocean cable may tell us that Paris, with every fiber quivering with the agony of impotent despair, writhes beneath the conquering heel of her cursed invader. Ere another moon shall wax and wane the brightest star in the galaxy of nations may fall from the zenith of her glory, never to rise again. Ere the modest violets of early spring shall open their beauteous eyes, the genius of civilization may chant the wailing requiem of the proudest nationality the world has ever seen, as she scatters her withered and tear-moistened lilies o'er the bloody tomb of butchered France. But, sir, I wish to ask if you honestly and candidly believe that the Dutch would have ever overrun the French in that kind of style if Gen. Sheridan had not gone over there and told King William and Von Moltke how he had managed to whip the Piegan Indians." (Great laughter.)

(Here the hammer fell)

(Many cries, " Go on !" " Go on.")

The Speaker—" Is there objection to the gentleman from Kentucky continuing his remarks ? The Chair hears none. The gentleman will proceed."

Mr. Knott—"I was remarking, sir, upon these vast ' wheat fields.' represented on this map in the immediate neighborhood of the buffaloes and the Piegans, and ·was about to say that the idea of there being these immense wheat fields in the very heart of a wilderness, hundreds and hundreds of miles beyond the utmost verge of civilization, may appear to some gentlemen rather incongruous—as rather too great a strain on the ' blankets' of veracity. But, to my mind, there is no difficulty in the matter whatever. The phenomenon is very easily accounted for. It is evident, sir, that the Piegans sowed that wheat there and plowed it in with buffalo bulls. (Great laughter.) Now, sir, this fortunate combination of buffaloes and Piegans, considering their relative positions to each other and to Duluth, as they are arranged on this map, satisfies me that Duluth is destined to be the beef market of the world.

" Here you will observe, (pointing to the map), are the buffaloes, directly between the Piegans and Duluth, and here, right on the road to Duluth, are the Creeks. Now, sir, when the buffaloes are sufficiently fat from grazing on those immense wheat fields, you see it will be the easiest thing in the world for the Piegans to drive them on down, stay all night with their friends, the Creeks, and go into Duluth in the morning. (Great laughter.) I think I see them now, sir, a vast herd of buffaloes, with their heads down, their eyes glaring, their nostrils dilated, their tongues out, and their tails curled over their backs, tearing along toward Duluth, with about a thousand Piegans on their grass-bellied ponies, yelling at their ·heels ! (Great laughter) On they come ! And as they sweep past the Creeks they join in the chase. and the way they all go, yelling, bellowing, ripping and tearing along. amid clouds of dust, until the last buffalo is safely penned in the stock yards of Duluth. (Shouts of laughter.)

" Sir, I might stand here for hours and hours, and· expatiate with rapture upon the gorgeous prospects of Duluth as depicted upon this map. But human life is too short, and the time of this House far too valuable to allow me to linger longer upon. the delightful theme. (Laughter.) I think every gentleman on this floor is as well satisfied as I am that Duluth is destined to become the commercial metropolis of the universe, and that this road should be built at once I am fully persuaded that no patriotic representative of the American people, who has a proper appreciation of the associated glories of Duluth and the St. Croix, will hesitate a moment to say that every able-bodied female in the land between the ages of eighteen and forty-five who is in favor of ' women's rights' should be drafted and set to work upon this great work without delay. (Roars of laughter) Nevertheless, sir, it grieves my very soul to be compelled to say that I cannot vote for the grant of lands provided for in this bill.

" Ah ! sir, you can have no conception of the poignancy of my anguish that I am deprived of the blessed privilege ! (Laughter.)

There are two insuperable obstacles in the way. In the first place, my constituents, for whom I am acting here, have no more interest in this road than they have in the great question of culinary taste now, perhaps, agitating the public mind of Dominica, as to whether the illustrious commissioners who recently left this capital for that free and enlightened republic would be better fricasseed, boiled or roasted (great laughter); and, in the second place, these lands which I am asked to give away, alas, are not mine to bestow! My relation to them is simply that of trustee to an express trust. And shall I ever betray that trust? Never, sir! Rather perish Duluth! (Shouts of laughter.) Perish the paragon of cities! Rather let the freezing cyclones of the bleak northwest bury it forever beneath the eddying sands of the St. Croix!" (Great laughter.)

PART IV.—OF SPEECH-MAKING IN GENERAL.

HAVING given the reader some idea of the three kinds of speeches mostly in vogue—for the set, or written oration, is confined now-a-days to the lecture-room or pulpit—we close by a chapter of detailed instruction.

No man should speak in public unless he have something to say, and a purpose to serve thereby. Nor should he speak unless he can say that something properly. Nor should he continue to speak after he has exhausted his subject. We therefore consider, first, the matter of the speech, secondly, the manner of the speech, and thirdly, the end of the speech

First, then, of the matter. There must be ideas, and one leading idea around which the rest should be grouped. This should be introduced by a brief exordium; and should be properly insisted on and sustained, but never entirely lost sight of. You speak to a certain end, whatever the subject, or whenever you speak. Let that be kept in mind from first to last. But do not attempt to do too much. If you are making a speech in opposition to a certain political policy, do not endeavor to expose all the errors of your opponents. Select the one which is most recent in public report; or most likely to arouse popular prejudice; or is of itself most enormous. Having presented its wrong in as terse language as possible, endeavor to show that it is not

so much due to the wickedness of your opponents as to the
inherent tendency of the system of public policy which they
support. Nothing is lost by attributing good motives to
your opponents. The hearer thinks you to be generous and
frank, which predisposes him to give you a fair hearing.
Then take up more particularly that part of their policy
connected with the particular subject under discussion. So
soon as you have made a strong point, and you see it has
told on the audience, do not weaken it by elaboration, but
go to another portion of the subject, or, if you find you have
made an effective hit, close without delay. If you are dis-
cussing a subject with others, you may proceed a little
differently. If they have made any points that are apt to
tell against your position, notice them after you have made
your own points, but do not be seduced to consider them
solely, or to devote too much time to their refutation, otherwise you will be forced into the defensive, which is always
disadvantageous.

Study to use the plainest and simplest words and phrases.
We do not mean by this that you should, in avoiding long
and ponderous words, fall into the error of using "slang"
expressions; but that you should take in preference words
of Saxon or Celtic rather than of Latin or Greek origin.
Say that the house was "burned," and not that it "fell
before the devouring elements;" say that the man was
' hanged," and not that he "suffered death by strangula-
tion;" say "milk" and not "the lacteal fluid"—in short,
use such words and phrases as are understood by the most
uncultured, and you will not injure yourself in the estimation of the learned. Otherwise, though you may astonish
the ignorant, you will be laughed at by people of common
sense, who are greater in number than some people suppose.

While we insist on using not only the simplest words, but
the fewest necessary to convey a meaning properly, we do
not advise that brevity should be carried to the extent of
barrenness. The use of words to an end is very much like
the use of money. It may be extravagant to expend
very little, and economical to spend very much. As that
is the best use of money which gets what we want for the
least expenditure, we use words best, when we just use

enough to convey our meaning clearly and elegantly, and no more.

Avoid quotations, unless they enforce a point, but above all keep clear of classical quotations, and scraps of foreign or dead languages. In a body composed of thoroughly-educated men you may air your learning a little, but not before a miscellaneous audience. If you do quote, however, see that it suits the time, and be not lugged in to show your memory.

Figures of rhetoric should be sparingly used, and some of them with more particular caution. Those most apt to be used by the inexperienced orator, are simile, metaphor, apostrophe and ecphonesis. Simile and metaphor differ in this—simile compares things, and metaphor identifies them. The latter is the more powerful, and in general preferable. " He is bold as a lion "—there is simile ; " he is a lion,"—that is metaphor. Either, however, should be sparingly employed, and should come naturally out of the management of the subject, and not be dragged in.

Apostrophe and ecphonesis differ in this—that apostrophe is an address to something or some one connected with the subject under consideration, while ecphonesis is a sudden exclamation, expressing some kind of emotion springing from the main subject. The latter is a very commonly used figure, and as it diverts the attention of the hearer from the main subject, its excess should be guarded against.

Antithesis is a figure of great value. By contrasting things or qualities directly opposite, it produces frequently a striking effect. One of the most remarkable specimens of antithesis, is to be found in one of the speeches of the celebrated Irish orator, Phillips, in which he speaks of the elder Napoleon as follows :

" Flung into life in the midst of a revolution that quickened every energy of a people who acknowledged no superior, he commenced his course, a stranger by birth, and a scholar by charity With no friend but his sword, and no fortune but his talents, he rushed in the list where rank, and wealth, and genius had arrayed themselves, and competition fled from him, as from the glance of destiny.

" He knew no motive but interest: acknowledged no criterion but success ; he worshipped no God but ambition, and with an eastern devotion, he knelt at the shrine of his idolatry. Subsidiary to this, there was no creed that he did not profess, there was no opinion that he did not promulgate; in the hope of a dynasty, he upheld the crescent; for the sake of a divorce, he bowed before the cross; the orphan of St. Louis, he became the adopted child of the republic; and with a parricidal ingratitude, on the ruins of both the throne and the tribune, he reared the throne of his despotism. A professed Catholic, he imprisoned the Pope; a pretended patriot, he impoverished the country; and in the name of Brutus, he grappled without remorse, and wore without shame. the diadem of the Cæsars.

"The whole continent trembled at beholding the audacity of his designs, and the miracle of their execution. Skepticism bowed to the prodigies of his performance; romance assumed the air of history; nor was there aught too incredible for belief, or too fanciful for expectation, when the world saw a subaltern of Corsica waving his imperial flag over her most ancient capitals. All the visions of antiquity became common-place in his contemplation; kings were his people; nations were his outposts; and he disposed of courts, and crowns, and camps, and churches. and cabinets, as if they were the titular dignitaries of the chess-board! Amid all these changes *he* stood immutable as adamant. It mattered little whether in the field, or in the drawing-room; with the mob, or the levee; wearing the. Jacobin bonnet, or the iron crown; banishing a Braganza. or espousing a Hapsburg; dictating peace on a raft to the Czar of Russia, or contemplating defeat at the gallows of Leipsic, he was still the same military despot.

"In this wonderful combination his affectations of literature must not be omitted. The jailer of the press. he affected the patronage of letters; the proscriber of books. he encouraged philosophy; the persecutor of authors, and the murderer of printers, he yet pretended to the protection of learning. the assassin of Palm. the silencer of De Stael, and the denouncer of Kotzebue; he was the friend of David, the benefactor of De Lille, and sent his academic prize to the philosopher of England.

"Such a medley of contradictions, and, at the same ₐtime, such an individual consistency, were never united in the same character. A Royalist, a Republican, and an emperor; a Mohammedan: a Catholic, and a patron of the synagogue; a subaltern and a sovereign: a traitor and a tyrant; a Christian and an infidel: he was, through all his vicissitudes, the same stern, impatient, inflexible original; the same mysterious, incomprehensible self;- the man without a model, and without a shadow."

Climax is a figure of great force, by which the speaker commences at the lowest or weakest, and gradually ascends to the highest or strongest points. But it is after all a story within a story; for a speech itself should be a climax, commencing with the weakest and closing at the strongest point.

"Time was, indeed, when the princes of a royal house, on returning from the chase, fired at the slaters at work on the house-tops of Paris, and laughed to see them fall. Time was when kings made battues of their unhappy subjects, and power coerced panting poverty till it stood hopelessly at bay or lay down in despair to die. But to-day all that has changed. The chase still goes on; now poverty coerces power. The hunters have become the hunted, and the game is royal."— *Thomas Dunn English.*

Personification, by which we give abstract matters or inanimate things a distinct personality, is often effectively introduced. In his speech in opposition to war measures, Josiah Quincy made a very fine use of this figure. He said:

" An embargo liberty was never cradled in Massachusetts Our liberty was not so much a mountain, as a sea nymph. She was free as air. She could swim, or she could run. The ocean was her cradle. Our fathers met her as she came, like the goddess of beauty, from the waves. They caught her as she was sporting on the beach. They courted her whilst she was spreading her nets upon the rocks· But an embargo liberty: a handcuffed liberty; a liberty in fetters; a liberty traversing between the four sides of a prison and beating her head against the walls, is none of our offspring. We abjure the monster. Its parentage is all inland."

These, and other figures of speech, are more to be spurned than employed, if the novice desires to make an effective speaker. He will be apt to think them fine, but this is an error. Even if excellent of themselves, they are apt to divert the mind of the auditors from the main question. Hence the best orators use them sparingly; and in any business speeches, never. In the latter, indeed, he is most effective who makes a plain statement, and occupies as little time as possible in doing it. The young and un-practiced orator does not make his speech, however, so much to gain a point, as to make a display. He is apt to think he has succeeded when some sally of his provokes laughter or wins applause. The practiced orator knows better; and is far better pleased if he obtain a close and earnest attention from his auditors. Hence he avoids mere display, and strives to give epigrammatic force to his sentences, and to condense as much as possible.

It is true that the style employed is to be modified a deal by the subject matter. In an oration on a set subject —in a lecture—in a sermon—or in a literary address, the style should be more ornate; and in a dinner-speech more

playful than in a business speech. But nowhere should the
ornament be cumbrous or excessive. It ceases to be ornament when it makes up the main matter. And elegance
may be had with the most sparing use of rhetorical figures,
or without them at all.

We recollect once attending the meeting of a council in
a country town, where a proposal to pave the main street
was under consideration. One member was in favor of
using cobble-stones for the purpose, and delivered quite a
long speech to show that this was the cheapest in the end,
that it would require less repair than other modes, and
would give the village quite a city-like appearance. His
remarks made some impression, though they rather tired
both the council, and the townsfolk who were listening to,
and interested in, the discussion. A quiet member, who
rarely spoke arose and answered him, substantially, and in
some part of our report, exactly, thus:

"Mr. Chairman: I have listened with proper attention to the
gentleman who has just sat down, and have weighed well all he has
said. I differ with him, and prefer that we should macadamize the
main street, for very plain reasons. The first cost of a thorough
macadamization is not only less, but it will be cheaper in the end.
Whether you cover the surface with broken stone, or with sand and
cobble stones, the surface must be properly graded in either instance
to receive this protecting coat. Thus far the cost is the same. Then
begins the difference. The gentleman admits that to haul the gravel
and to place the cobble-stones properly will cost more than to cover
the surface with eighteen inches of finely-broken stone. He thinks
that the cobble-stone pavement would remain inmovable, while the
macadamized surface would fall into ruts. If he will go to any city he
will discover that in a few months, more or less according to the
traffic, the cobble-stone pavement changes from its level to a succession
of hills and hollows; that the gravel in which the stones are bedded
retains moisture, and is acted on by frost which heaves the stones
above more or less out of place. Repairs are costly. They require
not only a resetting of the stone, but a readjustment of the gravel. The
macadamized road, if made as it ought to be, of small stones with
sharp edges, and without a mixture of gravel or clay, so that it will
bend by pressure, and pack into a natural drain from the surface, is
not upheaved by the frost; and any ruts that are formed can be easily
repaired with a few pecks of stones, if properly watched As to the
final reason in favor of cobble-stones, that it will give 'a city air' to
the main street, I presume this is meant as a sly bit of sarcasm, and
is not to be taken seriously. But if the gentleman be really in earnest,
I hope he will recall to his mind that we are not a city, and will not

become so by putting on a city air; and that he will remember the fate of the unlucky frog who undertook to swell to the size of an ox, and came to great grief in the attempt."

The council decided against the cobble-stones.

The main points of an effective speech are clearness of idea, precision of statement, simplicity of language, methodical arrangement, and a style of handling that hits the subject.

And, next, as to the manner of delivering the speech. We have already spoken about the attitude of the body, which should be free, natural and unconstrained; and about the avoidance of mechanical gesture. Some persons stand as immovable as stone posts, which is bad, but bad as it is, it is infinitely better than the trick of others who sway themselves violently back and forth, or use their arms as though they were the handles of a force-pump or the sails of a wind-mill.

We again call attention to distinctness of enunciation. Every word, syllable and sound, should be plainly articulated. While the voice should take the colloquial tone, the words should not be clipped, nor the sound of one run into the sound of another. This is an imperative rule, and can not be too much insisted on. In order to easily obey it, it is better to practice the vocal sounds, and repeat the labials, or lip sounds, dentals or teeth sounds, palatal or palate sounds and linguals, or tongue sounds, first separately and then in the words wherein they predominate. This done, the words wherein the dentals and linguals come together, and finally those in which the nasal sounds join the rest, should be practiced sedulously. Words terminating in *st*, or *t'st*, or *d'st*, if not perfectly pronounced annoy the ear, and often embarrass the speaker who feels his failure to give them in their full force.

The management of the voice requires careful study. Where the speech is narrative, or the statement of premises, the tone is that of ordinary conversation. Where the speaker warms with his subject, and becomes animated, the voice rises; if he touches upon a pathetic subject, the voice at the more affecting parts, sinks. If he indulges in humor, he gives the funny point with an expected quickness; if he

rises to the sublime, the voice takes on a monotone. Inflections and emphasis must be attended to, and closely
studied. Inflection is nothing more than the change of
tone—if it begin in a low tone, and end in a higher, that is
called the rising inflection ; and if it begin in a high tone and
end in a lower tone, that is the falling inflection. A
question is given with a rising, and an answer with falling
inflection. The only rule as to inflections which it is
requisite to follow closely is to let them come from your
own earnestness, and they will be natural, and so effective.
Emphasis, which is the dwelling upon particular words, and
not the mere uttering them in a louder tone—you may be
emphatic in a whisper—is to be carefully attended to. A
false emphasis might alter your entire meaning. Thus to
say—" *She* does not love me," infers that I am loved by
others but not by her—the emphasis on *she* really brings me
prominently forward ; but to say—" She does not love
me," intimates that she loves some one else, and makes her
the principal figure in the word-picture.

The great necessity of a young speaker is confidence, and
obliviousness to the audience. How often you hear two
well-informed men disputing on some topic, oblivious of the
fact that you are listening. Observe with what animation
and energy they make their points ! Notice how natural
are their tones, how correct their inflections, and how graceful their gestures ! Their language is simple, refined,
appropriate and forcible. But introduce thirty or forty
people who shall sit down and listen in grave silence to this
discussion. Notice how the spirits of the disputants sink ;
how their tones of voice change ; how irregular are the inflections, how uncertain the emphasis ; what stiffness replaces
the elegant gestures, and what embarrassment succeeds the
ease of manner ! The first requisite then for the student
of oratory is to learn to consider that he is engaged either
in a discussion with a friend, or in talking to some member
of his family. To do this more effectually, he should use a
colloquial tone of voice, and a familiar manner ; should
make no attempts at graceful gestures, or mere physical
eloquence, but accustom himself to facing a crowd. He
will find great help in this by looking at the farthest quiet

individual before him, and addressing him solely, keeping his eye on that one alone.

Practice speaking wherever you can. Do not disdain the debating society. The subjects chosen for discussion there are generally absurd, or at least trivial; but the practice is everything. Write out your views on any popular topic, and when you have done this, read it over again and again, prune it of all superfluous words;. cut out all adjectives not absolutely necessary; read it over again and again; declaim it in your chamber, and then—make lamplighters out of the manuscript. If you expect to or are desirous of making a speech on any subject, or are likely to be called to discuss it, read everything upon that subject you can find. Pore over, think over it in all its aspects, read both sides. You can not have too much knowledge. Knowledge aids you in matter—practice in manner. Read the speeches of Patrick Henry, the Randolphs, John Adams, Tristram Burgess (except his early ones), Josiah Quincy, Livingston, Clinton, Clay, Calhoun, Webster, Dallas, Douglass, Wise, Breckenridge, Wendell Phillips and Thaddeus Stevens in this country; and Chatham, Canning, Fox, Pitt, Curran, Burke, Grattan, Phillips, Cobden, Brougham, Peel, Bright, Palmerston, Disraeli and Gladstone in England. Practice the vocal sounds so as to obtain a distinct articulation. Make yourself master of your art by patient toil, abandoning the false notion that eloquence is a matter of inspiration. You may meet with some mortifications; but if you persevere you will be able to speak whenever called on, not only to your own satisfaction but to the pleasure of your auditors, and if you do not become the perfect orator, it lies in your power to be an elegant and effective public speaker.

And, finally, as to the end of the speech. When you have come to an end—, STOP!

PART V.—PRESENTATION SPEECHES SPECIALLY.

THIS chapter is a wheel within a wheel, and has been written after all the rest was in type. It is virtually a supplement—the result of an after suggestion; and, no matter where the publisher may put it, should be placed as an appendix.

An experienced friend, after reading the rest of the manus script, said : " Your little work is very practical in the main, and calculated to be serviceable, unless the reader be a noodle ; but—"

As he stopped here, and looked as wise as an owl, we inquired what followed the " but."

Said he, with the confidence of an oracle : " You should have devoted a chapter to Presentation Speeches. True, the man who reads your little treatise carefully, and digests the matter therein ought to be able to say what he has to say acceptably at least Ten to one, if he be the unhappy fellow who is to present something to some one on behalf of some others, or the unhappy fellow who is to get it, he won't. Give a few examples at least, of how the thing ought to be done—models for imitation."

Now that is the very thing we have avoided all through the book. We could cite some specimens to show how the thing has been done at times ; but they are not models.

We remember one. A silver goblet was to be given to a civic gentleman, by a number of admirers in his ward. The night of presentation came, and brought with it the donors, the donee, the goblet, and a basket of champagne.

After a moderate refreshment there was a dead pause. Then the chairman of the committee cleared his throat, and the auditors· breathlessly awaited the burst of eloquence from the silver-tongued orator. He struck an attitude— one arm thrust backward, the other extended and rather drooping—the exact position of an old-fashioned pump. Then he spoke :

" Alderman, that's the mug !"

The recipient advanced, took the goblet by the shank,

satisfied himself of its probable weight, set it down again, and replied in a timid way :

"Is that them ? Thank you. Gentlemen, let's imbibe."

And they imbibed.

We remember another. Here a watch was to be given another ward politician. The orator of the evening, commenced with a slight historical sketch of the various instruments. used for measuring and recording time—spoke of the dial of Ahaz, of the clepsydra, of ancient clocks, of the masterpiece at Strasburg, of "Nuremberg eggs," of wooden clocks, of escapements, of cylinders, of movements in general—a most cyclopedic summary of facts. From this he entered on a disquisition upon the value of time. Then he pounced upon the party to whom it was to be given, upon whom be pronounced a panegyric, and after a soul-stirring allusion to that variegated piece of bunting poetically known as the Star-Spangled Banner, and a passing reference to that mythical fowl usually called the American Eagle, wound up his hour and a quarter's work by handing over the chronometer. Then the donee began, and after occupying a half hour in explaining the emotions that agitated his manly bosom, pronounced a solemn vow that the watch would go down to his heirs as an evidence, &c. We presume that promise was kept—at least, about a year afterward, the party being then out of office and impecunious, it went to his "uncle's" as an evidence that he had effected a loan of fifty dollars on it.

On second thoughts we remember one more speech that was a very fair model in its way, and it was by a man who never had made a speech before in his life, but who achieved a social reputation of an enviable kind by that single effort.

The pupils of a well-known writing-master, at the close of the session, were so well pleased with the care taken by their teacher, that they subscribed and purchased for him a gold pen—a very neat affair, with a gold handle, studded with small diamonds. It cost twenty-five dollars—the share of each pupil being only about fifty cents. The class was made up mainly of clerks and workingmen ; and they

selected as their spokesman a young carpenter. In the
middle of the last lesson, the incipient orator, pen in hand,
rapped loudly on his desk. The teacher, who was engaged
in examining the copy of one of the pupils, looked up in
amaze.

" Mr. ——."

" Well ?" said the teacher inquiringly.

" Your pupils here have planned a little surprise for you, and they
hope it will be a pleasant one. They have obtained this pen, and have
commissioned me to present it to you in their name. In their behalf
I request you to accept it, not only as an acknowledgment of the care
you have bestowed on their instruction in penmanship, but as a token
of the good will they bear you, and as an evidence of how much they
appreciate your good temper, conscientiousness and the many other
good qualities they have found you to possess. Although it is a very
good pen, and a rather fine piece of workmanship, we expect you to
prize it less for its intrinsic value, than for the proof it gives you, that
where you thought you had only found fifty pupils, you find you have
made fifty friends."

The writing master was taken aback. The secret had
been well kept, and he was thoroughly surprised. He
stammered, hesitated, and at last said :

" Well, gentlemen, I accept it in the same spirit that it was offered,
and you may believe that I prize it very much. I *am* surprised, I am
a good deal more—I am delighted. It is not the first time that I have
received tokens like this from my pupils; but it always leaked out before,
and I was quite ready. This time I'm caught unprepared ; but I can
tell you that I am grateful in spite of the little embarrassment—not only
for the gift, which is something : but for the kind words, which are
more. I can shape letters better than I can utter words; but if I
have fifty friends here, and I know I have, each of the fifty has a warm
friend in me, and—"

Here he broke down, and they gave him three cheers;
and the whole affair wound up with a hand-shaking, and a
good time generally.

The great point of a presentation speech is the avoidance
of extraneous matter. The next most essential point is
that the words shall have an extempore air, and be cordial
but not too familiar, have no formality and yet not be
flippant, and show feeling without any mock sentiment.

It is quite common among parishioners now-a-days, when
a clergyman has been rather over-worked, to give him
leave of absence to travel, either to Europe or elsewhere;

and the wealthiest of his congregation in that case make up a purse to defray his traveling expenses. This is usually presented at a vestry or committee meeting, or at the parsonage, or rectory. As the clergyman is the head of the spiritual family, the members of his parochial charge approach him with more external marks of respect than ward politicians bestow on their leader. Thus the spokes-man may say:

" Reverend and dear sir: Your parishioners are sorry to part with you, even for a brief time, and more sorry that your health, broken down in the service of our Divine Master, and in your ministering to the spiritual needs of your flock, requires change of air and scene to restore it. We desire to see you back among us as you were, ready to enter with renewed vigor on your labors. In order that your mind may be free from any anxiety about pecuniary matters, and you may thus derive the most unalloyed pleasure from your travels, a few of your parishioners have taken the liberty of making up a small purse for your use. We know of no reason why your children in the faith should not take care of the mere physical wants of their spiritual father, and we ask you to accept this, as some token of the esteem and reverence we bear for you ; and with it to carry away our warm hopes for a pleasant voyage and a joyous return."

Or he may say, more briefly :

" Reverend and dear sir: We regret to lose you even for a time from our midst, but as we know you have been overworked of late, and require a slight vacation, we bear our parting as an unpleasant necessity. You must not go too scantily provided with means, and we expect you to permit us to discharge some part of our many debts to you, by this slight contribution which I am directed to place in your hands. The ties which join us are so tender and intimate, and you have been so completely the head of our spiritual household, that we claim it as our right to give, and your duty to accept, this little mark of our friendship and veneration "

Or, more briefly still :

" If you must leave us, brother ——, you must not go on your journey too scantily provided. Pray add this mite to your means of travel, and when you visit the scenes where our Lord lived and suffer-ed, remember pleasantly and affectionately your children in the faith whose hearts go forth with you in all your wanderings."

A recent convention of the editors of New York state was marked by a pleasant little presentation episode, Mr. A. O. Bunnell, of the Dansville *Advertiser*, being the re-cipient of a handsome cane, a compliment from his editorial

brethren. Mr. MacArthur, the spokesman, in the words
of the Watertown *Daily Times,* "then stepped forward and
confronted Mr. Bunnell with a weapon in his hand which
looked suspiciously like a cane."

He proceeded to speak as follows :

" Sir, I am happy that it is my pleasant duty to address the *hand-
somest man in the state.* I am delighted, sir, that to me is deputed
the duty of caning you on this occasion ; and while I am not very
strong in eloquence and power, I feel that I am able to cane you.
You have discharged the duties of your position far more ably than
any other member of our association could have done, and I certainly
know that your hand-writing is a great improvement on Horace
Greeley's. I assure you, sir, that the editorial association, of which
you have been so long an ornament, feel that in presenting this cane
to you, they but feebly acknowledge what you have done for them.
Sir, I assure you that this is a gold-headed cane. My only grief in
parting with it is that gold is very scarce in our profession, and we
wish to hold on to it as long.as possible. Sir, I will not prolong these
remarks. I am happy to be permitted to present this to you. I hope
it will be many years before you find it necessary to rely upon this as
your chief staff of life."

Mr. Bunnell replied in the following manner:

" Mr. MacArthur and brethren of the Association, I do not know
what to say to-night. Your confidence in my integrity and ability,
which has been expressed year after year, by re-electing me to a
position responsible, and sometimes delicate, has touched my heart
very tenderly. I wish I had better deserved this testimonial. But
this renewed and intensified expression of your esteem has taken me
by storm. This whole affair, this scene about me to-night seems like
a wonderful dream of fairyland, and I know of but one way to account
for it. One of the finest writers of the English language has said that
' the world is curved round about with heaven. Its great, blue arches
bend low on every hand. and how one can get out of the world without getting into heaven is, to us, a physical mystery.' It seems to me
that somehow I have got out of the world and got into heaven ; and
as an editor I never expected to get into heaven, I don't know what
to do or say now that I am there. Gentlemen, I can only thank you
for this beautiful and costly testimonial, and I hope I may be better
worthy of it than I have been in the past."

Social gifts are usually attended with a little speech-
making, for the family and its friends require something of
the kind, as a concession to the general love of gab. This
should have even less form than the parochial or the political gift speech. Thus at a wedding-breakfast, the uncle
of the bride may desire to give her a watch. He seizes the

opportunity after the guests have broken the edge of appetite, to interpose in the first lull of chat, by a direct address to the bride :

"My dear Mrs. ——."

Of course, the lady starts at the mention of her new name, and looks up, blushing and all that.

" My dear Mrs. ——: You are about to set out on two journeys, one, a marriage-tour, which will end in a short time, and the other, marriage, which only ends with the life of one of you. In all journeys, if you want to get along smoothly, you must be promptly, as the railroad people say—' on time.' To be on time, you must have a faithful watch. I believe you have a rather good one, but here is one that I think to be better. Be kind, enough to take it, with the good wishes of your uncle, and all of your friends; and remember that though you owe your first duty and your supremest love to your husband, your new condition has not separated you from your old connections, but merely introduced another into our family. God bless you, my dear child, and give you and your husband many and happy years."

Fire-engine companies, militia organizations, and benevolent societies have their little presentations to make, and they are often puzzled how to get through the ceremonies properly. It is rather difficult to get up any eloquence over a silver speaking-trumpet, and even the subject of a sword has been so worn out. that anything novel is out of the question. But the speaker should remember that the thing presented has nothing to do with the talk. It is only necessary that it should be appropriate. To give a soldier a gold pen, or present a peaceable little tailor with a Toledo blade, would be impertinent, at least. It is the motive of the gift, and the feelings which prompt the givers, with which the speaker has to deal.

If the speaker is troubled as to matter, let him think on the golden word "brevity." If he take the fire-trumpet in one hand, and the hand of the recipient in the other, and say :

"My dear sir: Your fellow-members, who are also your personal friends, have commissioned me to present you this trumpet, as a mark of their respect for your efficiency as a fireman, and of their friendship for you as a man,"

—he will do very well. If he chooses to add:

" It is a very pleasant duty to fulfill, I assure you ; for I share all their feelings to the very utmost,"

—or words to that effect, he may with propriety; but he had better stop with the first set.

Frequently at school exhibitions, where books, or other testimonials, are given to pupils who have distinguished themselves by scholarship or deportment, or both, these are accompanied by a little speech This speech, which covers all the gifts, is mostly of the namby-pamby, goody-goody style, and neither pleases the audience nor satisfies the boys, which last are better judges of oratory than their elders are apt to think.   The usual style is to say:

"Master Jacky Goodboy: Your assiduity in the acquisition of knowledge and your uniformly correct deportment during the period of scholastic duties, has rendered this acknowledgment—"

And so on, *ad nauseam.* Jacky takes the book and goes down, with a wink, to his comrades, which, in the language of Winkland, means—" What an old pump !"

It would be much better to say to him:

" John Goodboy: This book, which I hope will interest and amuse you, is presented to you because you have been attentive to your studies, and have behaved yourself in school properly.   Continue the same industry and good manners during life, and you will no doubt be a successful man—at all events, you will never have occasion to reproach yourself with idleness or bad manners, and that is a kind of success in itself."

Or the speaker may say simply :

" This book is given you as an acknowledgment of your attention to your lessons and your good behavior during school hours.   Take it, with the good wishes of your teacher."

And this last form expresses everything. The boys will understand it, and respect the teacher, and then the Winkland dialect may be translated—" Ain't he a nice old fellow ?"

In the matter of sword presentations, as a general thing, some practiced speech-maker is chosen to do the talking. Where this is not the case, the task is by no means difficult if the general rule referred to is borne in mind Say as little about the weapon as possible. Allude slightly to war. Make no reference to turning the blade into a pruning hook. Let the Roman Mars and the Greek Ares remain in their respective mythologies.   If the gift arise from mere good-feeling and admiration, say so ; if because the recipient has distinguished himself on some martial occasion, say that. In fact, the object of the speech is to show that you give the sword from personal feeling, or from a sense of duty ; and the words should express the object plainly, and no more.

Thus, in the first instance :

"Colonel ——: You have now been in command of this regiment long enough for your subalterns and the rank and file, to appreciate fully your particular attention to your duties; your interest in the prosperity of the force, and your peculiar fitness for command. They desire you to accept this sword, whose blade is without a flaw and has a matchless temper, and I give it in their name, with the hope that you will not only prize it from its beauty and serviceable qualities, but as one of the proofs that all under your command have learned the fact that a good officer may preserve the most rigid discipline, and yet retain the respect, esteem and warm affection of all his officers and men.".

Or, in the second instance :

"Captain ——: You may be modest enough not to recall to your mind the day at (here name the battle,) when you led the charge so effectively on the enemy's line. But our memory is more active ; and as your old comrades and friends, we present you with this sword, to show somewhat our appreciation of your gallantry and worth. Take it. We hope you may never have occasion to use it—for as we have been in battle, we know that war is a duty at times, to be fulfilled when it comes, but never to be sought for. But should the occasion arise when this blade has to be used, we commit it to you with the full confidence that you will not draw it without cause, but when once drawn you will not sheath it until the glitter of its blade has lit the way to triumph."

This last sentence has a rather warm figure, only to be used if there be plenty of champagne about. It might be better to say :

"And will not then sheath it till the occasion for its use has past "

But this depends a good deal on the quantity and nature of the liquor lying about loose.

And talking of liquor, reminds us of another kind of presentation—the gift of a water-bucket, to a temperance advocate which it befell us once to have to speak for. It was a very small bucket of silver—about three inches by four, meant as a butter-dish ; but the idea of the gift was not ours, and others are responsible for the incongruity. As near as we remember the speech was thus :

"Doctor A——: A number of your friends, and friends of the cause, have requested me to act as their spokesman on this occasion. They ask me to present to you in their name this token of their ad- miration for your personal good qualities, and for the efficient and earnest way you have so long advocated the principles of total ab- stinence. It is, you see, a water-bucket, and so small as to seem almost a satire on those who advocate large draughts of cold water. But the truth is, while to the external glance it is a water-bucket, to the internal view it is a butter-dish. The cold water is to be outside and not in. Thus you see that the article is to represent the two most potent agents in the total abstinence reformation—the pump and the cow. There is a hidden meaning in it, I fancy. You are a bachelor—more shame to you. You have no wife, or you wouldn't love any *but her*, and a butter-dish is appropriate enough. And the shape conveys our wishes for your long life. You may kick at vice, kick at intemperance, kick at all the excesses that disfigure and des- troy society ; but out of sheer regard for the proprieties of life you can't kick at a thing given to you with the warmest feelings of friend- ship, and therefore cannot *kick the bucket*."

There was nothing but cold water about, but from the uproar that followed, a bummer who was listening outside was heard to exclaim : "There's them teetotalers agoin' it —they re drunk again!"

HANDBOOK OF VENTRILOQUISM.

'This little work, though only recently published, has met with an extensive sale, and the testimony of readers and the press fully sustains our claim that it is the best treatise on the subject that has been published. In all previous publications purporting to treat this subject. there has been really very little practical information given ; and though perhaps in some cases readable enough, the main object which the purchaser desired, instruction in the art, was not attained. The instructions in the present volume are very plain and minute, founded on common sense, and by their aid any one with patience and practise may become a ventriloquist, as the learner, after a few lessons, is able to ex ercise this power in some measure. The course of study and practice is by no means disagreeable or tiresome. The book also gives instructions for making

THE MAGIC WHISTLE,

A little instrument easily made, at no cost, for imitating birds, animals, insects, and quite a number of other amusing imitations. Considerable practice is required to enable one to use the whistle satisfactorily. The entertainment to be derived from it, however, will amply repay the labor.

" It is really a valuable aid to those desirous of acquiring the art, and the instructions and explanations are so simple and explicit that there is no difficulty in understanding them. It is prepared with much more care than we should expect in such a low-priced work, and makes a handy pocket companion.' "—*Boston Wide World.*

" This little manual contains simple and explicit instructions for acquiring the art of ventriloquism. Couched in language which a child can understand, the rules are so few and so easy that a little practice will enable any one to produce the most wonderful vocal illusions."—*New York Atlas.*

" The author appears to have labored faithfully to explain the mysteries of the art, and to initiate the learner therein." —*Yankee Blade.*

☞ This, and all other works in our list, will be sent post paid on receipt of price.

Price Fifteen Cents.

SECRETS WORTH KNOWING.

A COMPLETE HAND-BOOK OF USEFUL KNOWLEDGE.

Contains innumerable receipts for the manufacture of all kinds of useful articles, including Patent Medicines, Perfumery, Hair Oils, Pomatums, Dyes, Restoratives, Powders, Washes, Cements for filling Teeth, Cosmetics, Toilet Articles, Common and Fancy Soaps, Popular Beverages, including a large number of delicious ones just suited to the hot weather, healthful and cheap ; Candies of all kinds, including all the new and popular kinds ; Recipes for Housekeepers, Hundreds of Useful Articles which are needed in every household, and a large number of articles that can be manufactured and sold at a good profit. This is no cheap trash, like many works that have been issued, but a carefully-compiled volume of **100** pages, in neat form for preservation. It will be found of great value for reference, as you can find recipes on almost every subject on which you desire to be posted. Price, only **25** cents. A single receipt may prove worth the entire cost of the work.

The value of this book may be judged from the fact that single recipes contained therein are sold at from 25 cents to $5, and in some instances even more. Thousands of persons are making money by the manufacture of articles, recipes for which will be found in this book ; witness the success of Spalding's Glue, the various roofing cements, indelible inks, cordials, and the innumerable articles which everybody needs and will buy, and which can be manufactured and sold at a good profit. We have no wish to exaggerate—we do not offer any one a " fortune for 25 cents "—but we do offer to tell our readers how things can be made at small expense, which are selling every day in all parts of the country for five or ten times their original cost. A man of our acquaintance in this city is making several thousand dollars a year by making Lemon Syrup. " Secrets Worth Knowing" will tell you how to make it. We might multiply instances, but have not room.

" SECRETS WORTH KNOWING."—A neat and well-printed *brochure* of some 100 pages, with this title is before us. It is a receipt book, but occupies a field somewhat different from any other work. Though cooking receipts are given they form but a small portion of the contents. Receipts, in the discretion of the purchaser, are given for almost every imaginable article, from patent or non-professional medicines to liquid glue, and no doubt large profits could be realized by any one from the manufacture of many articles here enumerated. The receipts for wine-making will do much to aid in substituting harmless home-made beverages for poisonous " doctored " liquors. It is a good book for reference, being evidently prepared in good faith, and should be in the hands of all interested in its subject matter. Haney & Co., of this city, publish it.—*New Yorker*.

" SECRETS WORTH KNOWING."—We have received this popular hand-book of universal knowledge. It contains over 2,000 valuable receipts. It is also a reliable guide for the preparation of all kinds of medicine. The remarkable cheapness of the work places it within the reach of all. Price, 25 cents. Wm. U. Hess has it for sale.—*Columbia (Penn.) Spy*.

" SECRETS WORTH KNOWING."—A pamphlet with this title, containing over 2,000 recipes for articles in various branches of manufacture, some of them extremely valuable, all afforded for the low price of 25 cents, has been published by J. C Haney & Co., 1 9 Nassau street, N. Y.—*Brooklyn Daily Union*.

* * * It contains over 2,000 receipts for making everything that one can conceive of. It seems to be prepared with great care, and is believed to be reliable. —*Topeka State Record*.

" SECRETS WORTH KNOWING"—Containing over 2,000 valuable receipts for the manufacture of articles of every-day use, and a reliable guide for the preparation of all the popular Patent Medicines of the day.—*Orlean Times*.

* * * The book should be in the possession of every one.—*Manheim Sentinel*.

☞ The book can be had of any Bookseller or Newsdealer, or we will send a copy, post-paid, to any address, for 25 cents.

Dealers will find it a quick-selling work. Trade supplied by all wholesale houses. Wholesale and retail cash orders will be attended to promptly.

THE TAXIDERMIST'S MANUAL.

Good Books for Self-Improvement.

SELF CURE of STAMMERING and STUTTERING.

Gives a clear and full explanation of the most successful modes of treatment, and enables the stammerer to cure himself without surgical operation or machinery, and without *cost*. **25** cents.

Self-Cure of Debility, Consumption, Dyspepsia, Nervous Diseases, &c.

This book is issued in response to an urgent demand. It tells the real nature of many things which have been grossly misrepresented by unprincipled medical pretenders, enabling the patient himself to ascertain his real condition, to distinguish between the important and the unimportant "symptoms," and to escape the extortions of quacks, and to cure himself by simple means, within reach of all without any expense. The need of a reliable book of this kind, while lying and vulgar pamphlets are scattered in millions by quacks, is evident. Our book is simple in language, explicit in all directions, and founded on the very soundest medical science. The means of treatment are always safe, avoiding all the dangers of empirical tampering and proprietary "nostrums." and are the most approved and successful of the regular faculty. They are the surest, safest, speediest, simplest and most thorough means of cure that are known. **75** cents.

RAPID RECKONING.

A system of performing arithmetical calculations with almost instantaneous quickness. This system was the key to the wonderful performances of the "Lightning Calculator," whose exhibitions were the marvel of thousands. He sold the secret at $1 per copy. Our book is much enlarged, with many interesting additions. Any one can learn and practice. Valuable to bookkeepers, teachers, students and all business men. **25** cents.

IMPROVEMENT OF MEMORY.

Shows how to make a bad memory good and a good memory better; the system enabling all to strengthen their memories and often display a power which is surprising. **15** cents.

EMPLOYMENT SEEKERS' GUIDE.

Designed to present the advantages and disadvantages of various trades and professons, advice on investing money, starting in business, obtaining employment, qualifications necessary for different purposes, deceptive undertakings, comparative value of different schemes for money making, and much useful and interesting matter, especially valuable to the young and inexperienced. enabling them to make best use of their abilities and avoid snares of sharpers and quicksands of business. **25** cents. In press.

HANEY'S ART OF TRAINING ANIMALS.

This book is a complete guide, the only one fully and specially treating the subject. and *gives more information* about the training of animals *in single chapters* than other *entire books*. Has the most approved methods of the most celebrated and successful trainers, thoroughly initiating the reader into all the secrets of the profession, exposing various bogus "charms," &c., sold to the credulous at high prices, and telling, in fact, *everything* connected with the art of breaking, taming, and training all animals. Besides containing a vast amount of information which will be of real interest and value to farmers and others, it is full of attraction for boys. It not only explains how all the marvelous feats displayed by trained animals at public exhibitions are taught, but shows how many amusing and surprising tricks may be taught by any boy to dogs ponies or other pets. One gentleman writes us that his boys have organized quite an interesting amateur circus with their pet animals, who have been taught many of the best tricks by following its instructions, and he proposes getting them a little tent.

"Horses firing off pistols, answering questions by nodding or shaking their heads, dancing dogs and bears, performing canary birds and fleas, and the like, are 'some pumpkins,' but how about those wonderful dogs who play dominoes; select from a heap any article therein they are ordered to, and give it to any person named; dogs who spell words by selecting lettered cards, or answer questions, tell your age or your fortune by the same means? Or the monkeys who enact little dramas, personating the characters in a manner to shame many of their human compeers? Or seals who play the hand-organ? Fortunately for the excited juvenile community, a certain Mr. Haney has come to the rescue with a full exposition of the Art of Training Animals, explaining these and hundreds of other feats, to the infinite joy of every boy who can now convert his own pets into a circus troupe at a cost about equal to a single admission to the 'big tent.'"—*N. Y. Evening Express.*

"There is scarcely an animal which has escaped our author's clutches, and he has certainly presented a vast amount of interesting information touching their character and tuition. Not only are the ordinary feats of the circus explained, but the most intricate tricks exhibited by some few renowned 'stars' among animal performers."—*Turf, Field, and Farm.*

"The performances of trained animals have always been painful rather than interesting to us, from the thought of the amount of suffering necessary to bring it about. The author of this book, however, tells us how to train or pet dogs, cats, horses etc., to very wonderful feats at only the expense of a little patience and skill.—*Little Corporal, Chicago.*

"Even those who do not seek it for its information will find it agreeable to read."—*Providence Press.*

"A large variety of information, truly, to be embodied in a single book at so small a price."—*New England Farmer.*

"The raising and training of pets is a pleasurable occupation, and one that we would like to see encouraged among our farmers' boys."—*Prairie Farmer.*

"Mingles with its clear directions a number of pleasant incidental facts, pleasantly told."—*N. Y. Day Book.*

"Furnishes very entertaining reading."—*Phila Daily Ledger.*

"Will entertain both old and young."—*Advance.*

"We have to thank Mr. Haney for many facts regarding animals beyond the mere trainer's province, which it is interesting to know."—*Boston Am. Union.*

210 Pages. 60 Illustrations. Paper Covers 50 cts.; Boards, 75 cts.; Cloth $1.

For sale by booksellers generally, or sent by mail, post-paid, on receipt of price.

THE aim of this little book is to furnish a cheap and reliable handbook on the subjects of Hunting, Trapping, Fishing, and the preparation of Skins and Furs, with such other information on kindred subjects as shall be useful to the reader, whether he proposes to follow our instructions as a source of profit or merely for amusement. It is not pretended that this little volume gives *everything* of interest or value—no one book has ever done so, even among those costing from three to five dollars. Our book will, perhaps, be more serviceable in the majority of cases than even these costly works, because just the information most universally desired—the *cream*, we may say, of the bulky volumes.

While these elaborate treatises answer the demands of luxurious readers, and those desiring complete libraries, there is an urgent want of a cheap and reliable work devoted to the *practical* branches of these subjects. It is simple truth to say that this want has never been supplied. Mere *low price* is not "cheapness," and if an instruction book cannot be *relied* on it is dear even as a gift. That *no reliable* book of this kind has heretofore been published at less than one dollar is to be easily ascertained by any one who cares to devote the money to purchase, and the time to examine, the various things advertised. The most pretentious of these seems to have secured all the *un*reliable recipes floating around, the very ones most highly extolled in the book are certain "charms" exposed long ago in Haney's Journal, and known by all competent to judge to be just the contrary to what is claimed for them in this "guide." The concoctor of that collection we can only acquit of deliberate falsehood and fraud, by supposing him too ignorant to be aware of their real character. We believe in addition to their worthlessness, that, in nearly every state, their use will subject the credulous victim not only to heavy fine but a probable sojourn in prison. Whatever is good in the book is certainly not original, and is better obtained in its original sources.

System of increasing speed to which Dexter owes his supremacy, with much useful information for all horsemen. Endorsed by Robert Bonner, Esq. **50 cts**

College Scrapes.—The best expose of college life and college fun ever issued. A rare treat full of queer and amusing incidents, jolliest book out, with many comic illustrations, **15 cts.**

Houdin the Conjuror.—His remarkable life, amusing and startling adventures and marvelous feats. Large octavo, illustrated. / **50 cts**

Taxidermist's Manual.—A complete and practical guide to collecting, preparing and preserving all kinds of birds, animals, insects, reptiles &c. **50 cts.**

Fun Everlasting.— A mammoth collection of the very best original and selected comic stories, jokes, witticisms, puns, funny yarns, laughable adventures, burlesques, and a general melange of jolly rollicking good humor, with over one hundred humorous illustrations by celebrated artists. We believe no one can fail to be well pleased and enjoy many a hearty laugh over its endless fund of amusement. **15 cts**

Book of Advertised Wonders.—A collection of the various arts, secrets, money making schemes, "patent" rights, recipes, &c., of all kinds and qualities sold by traveling speculators and by newspaper and circular advertisers, embracing much that is really valuable, much that is worthless, and much that is fraudulent; with notes explanatory of the real character of each, which will save costly fees to speculators and in many cases waste of time and material. Collected at an expense of over $250. 100 pages. **50 cts**

Self Cure of Stammering.—*Not* an advertising pamphlet but a concise and plain exposure of the most approved and successful methods of Self Treatments, with exposure of empirical and dangerous devices. **25 cts.**

Self Cure of Debility, Consumption, Dyspepsia, Nervous-ness, &c.—Advertises no doctor or medicine, but gives plain, instructions for self cure by simple means within reach of all which will cost *nothing*, and are the surest, safest, and quickest methods of cure. Dangers of advertised modes of treatment, quack nostrums, &c., are pointed out. **75 cts**

Sign, Carriage and Decorative Painting.— An entirely new practical work, giving full and plain instructions in these and kindred branches; *only* book treating FRESCO. This book is entirely distinct from our "Painter's Manual," by a different author, and is designed especially for those who wish a book treating *specially* the subjects of Sign, Carriage and Decorative Painting. It is believed it will prove as popular and useful with those persons as has our "Painter's Manual" with the profession in general. Illustrated. **50 cts**

Soap-Makers' Manual.—Plain and practical guide for the manufacture of plain and fancy soaps, hard and soft soaps, washing fluids, medicinal soaps, etc. for the guidance of families and manufacturers. Has exposures of the adulterations practiced, and illustrations of most approved machinery for those desiring to operate medium sized works. Has best American, English, French and German formulas. **25 cts**

Handbook of Dominoes.—Gives full instructions in all games with Dominoes, including new and popular Foreign ones. **15 cts.**

Horse Shoers' Manual.—Includes preparation of foot, choice of shoes and their preparation, fitting, filing, nails and nailing, shoeing with leather, cutting, removing, etc. Plain and practical, with numerous engravings; also includes Youatt's Treatise on Diseases of the Horse's Foot. **25 cts**

Home Recreations, or How to Amuse the Young Folks.— Designed to afford fresh and agreeable entertainment for juvenile parties, holidays, and the home circle. Illustrated. **25 cts**

Spirit Mysteries Exposed.—A complete and plain exposition of all the marvelous feats of the "spirit rappers" and "mediums," Davenports, Hume, &c. So fully laid bare that any one can perform. Illustrated. **15 cts.**

Book of Alphabets.—For use of Painters, Sign-writers, Draughtsmen, &c. **50 cts**

Watchmakers' and Jewelers' Manual.—Latest and most approved methods and secrets of the trade, embracing watch and clock cleaning and repairing, tempering in all its grades, making tools, compounding metals, soldering, plating, etc, with plain instructions for beginners, etc. **25 cts**

☞ For sale by booksellers generally, or sent by mail, postage paid, on receipt of marked price.

JESSE HANEY & CO. 119 Nassau Street New York.

By means of circulars and newspaper advertisements a thriving business is done in selling recipes, rights to make or use wonderful discoveries, and various secrets, &c. Some of them are good, some worthless, some fraudulent. Many invest a few shillings or dollars out of mere curiosity or in hopes of money making or gaining knowledge. We have collected at cost of over $250 all the prominent of these advertised things. Their sellers we find have no exclusive right to them, so we propose to give our **$250** worth to the public in a neat little book which we call the

BOOK OF ADVERTISED WONDERS.

This gives the good, bad and indifferent, but with comments explaining the real character of each. The following list will give an idea of the contents:

It tells you how to make vinegar in ten hours from molasses, sorghum cider, &c., without drugs or chemicals; American gin without any distillation at 16 cts. per pint; Premium mead; Ale without malt or hops; Cure for asthma; Imitation cogniac brandy equal to finest French genuine; Glycerine cement; Chinese art of dwarfing trees; How to raise the vinegar plant; Bee-keeper's secret for securing fertilization of young queens by any drones desired; How to secure nearly double the usual product in artificial fish raising; Chemical paint, durable and odorless, of any color, without oil; Great water-proof varnish for boots and shoes; Kapnophyte, the new departure in fertilizers; Great art of chemicalizing manure; Great vegetable remedy for burns, scalds, &c.; Food for mocking birds; Death to the cotton worm; India-rubber cement.

Nickel plating without a battery; Art of saw-filing; Remedy for love of strong drink; Hunter's secrets and private guide to trappers; "Mad-stones," how to find, how to prepare and how to use the great natural remedy for bites of poisonous or rabid animals; Seltzer aperient; Excelsior axle grease; Art of sharpening saws; Magical British washing powder; Printer's indispensable, improving and drying inks of all kinds and colors—greatest help to good printing ever invented; Imperial fly paper, or "catch 'em alive oh!" Soluble blues, or liquid bluing; English harness blacking; Preserving grapes in their natural condition all winter; How to make brandy from shavings; Apple butter without apples; Old orchards made new, Kainite, or tree medicine; Safety gunpowder; 100 pounds of soap for one dollar; How to keep apples fresh and sound all winter; Tyler's permeating powder, How to restore vitality of seeds; Hunter's Secret; How to make honey from tomatoes; Chinese art of catching fish; Infallible remedy for potato rot; Liquid black lead polish; "All farmers and horse owners;" Barrel of soft soap for 75 cts.; Dead shot for rose slugs; Scrofula ointment; Rat killing without traps or poison; Baking powder; Maple sugar without maple trees.

Fifty methods of making money; Fire-proof paint; Premium black writing ink; Magic copying; Vegetable salve; Counterfeit detector; Art of painting on glass; Celebrated chemical compound; Hunter's secret; Soft soap; Starch polish. Cider better than from apples and not intoxicating; Rheumatic liniment; Magnetic ointment; Indian pills; Red ink; Blue ink; Indelible ink, without preparation; Luminous ink; Red ruling ink; Yellow ink; Invisible ink; Water-proof Composition; Gunpowder; Shaving soap; Hard solder; Soft solder; Silver plating fluid; Great pain extractor; Matches; Horse taming; Oil-paste blacking; Metals preserved from rust; Sealing wax; Cologne water; Hair restorative; Curling liquid for the hair; Excelsior hair oil; Celebrated tooth powder; Cough syrup; Universal liniment; Brick paint; Wood paint; Best varnish; Leather varnish; Almond soap; Fancy soap; Non-explosive burning fluid; Florida water; Macassar oil; Lavender perfumed water; Buffalo oil.

Sun-light oil; Corassa compound; Inman's cure for nervous weakness, &c.; Clover vinegar; Curing pork without brine; Sure and safe remedy for warts; Electric blacking; How to add 50 per cent. to yield of grain at trifling labor and expense; Hardening gloss for printer's inks; Whiskers in six weeks; Beautiful art of transferring any kind of pictures to glass; Great American washing fluid; Liebig's great fertilizer; Gilding without a battery; Water witching, or art of finding hidden water, oil or other valuable fluids beneath the ground, with the forked switch; Yeast from grape leaves; How to soften hard water; Butter without milk or cream—artificial butter which cannot be told from genuine; Chinese cure for neuralgia; Pain paint; Artificial fruit syrups for soda water, and a secret for adding largely to profits; Meat preserving in hot weather; Bordeaux wine imitation; Art of waterproofing cloth; Phycometic fascination, or art of soul charming; Colored fires for theatrical and other purposes; Boiler incrustation preventive; Vegetable cure for hydrophobia; Egg preserving secret; Laundry secrets; Art of pickling meat in one day.

☞ In neat 12mo volume of 100 pages,   **PRICE FIFTY CENTS.**

CPSIA information can be obtained
at www.ICGtesting.com
Printed in the USA
BVHW05s1446040518
515207BV00009B/200/P